MW00982191

J. Fredericks Volkwein, *State University of New York at Albany*
EDITOR-IN-CHIEF

Larry H. Litten, *Consortium on Financing Higher Education,
Cambridge, Massachusetts*
ASSOCIATE EDITOR

Mobilizing for Transformation: How Campuses Are Preparing for the Knowledge Age

Donald M. Norris
Strategic Initiatives, Inc.

James L. Morrison
University of North Carolina at Chapel Hill

EDITORS

Number 94, Summer 1997

JOSSEY-BASS PUBLISHERS
San Francisco

MOBILIZING FOR TRANSFORMATION: HOW CAMPUSES ARE PREPARING FOR
THE KNOWLEDGE AGE
Donald M. Norris, James L. Morrison (eds.)
New Directions for Institutional Research, no. 94
Volume XXIV, Number 2
J. Fredericks Volkwein, Editor-in-Chief

New Directions for Institutional Research is indexed in *College Student
Personnel Abstracts, Contents Pages in Education,* and *Current Index to Jour-
nals in Education* (ERIC).

Microfilm copies of issues and articles are available in 16mm and 35mm,
as well as microfiche in 105mm, through University Microfilms Inc., 300
North Zeeb Road, Ann Arbor, Michigan 48106-1346.

ISSN 0271-0579   ISBN 0-7879-9851-6

NEW DIRECTIONS FOR INSTITUTIONAL RESEARCH is part of The Jossey-Bass
Higher and Adult Education Series and is published quarterly by Jossey-
Bass Inc., Publishers, 350 Sansome Street, San Francisco, California
94104-1342 (publication number USPS 098-830). Periodicals postage
paid at San Francisco, California, and at additional mailing offices. POST-
MASTER: Send address changes to New Directions for Institutional Re-
search, Jossey-Bass Inc., Publishers, 350 Sansome Street, San Francisco,
California 94104-1342.

SUBSCRIPTIONS cost $54.00 for individuals and $90.00 for institutions,
agencies, and libraries.

EDITORIAL CORRESPONDENCE should be sent to J. Fredericks Volkwein,
Institutional Research, Administration 241, State University of New York
at Albany, Albany, NY 12222.

Photograph of the library by Michael Graves at San Juan Capistrano by
Chad Slattery © 1984. All rights reserved.

TCF Manufactured in the United States of America on Lyons Falls Turin
Book. This paper is acid-free and 100 percent totally chlorine-free.

THE ASSOCIATION FOR INSTITUTIONAL RESEARCH was created in 1966 to benefit, assist, and advance research leading to improved understanding, planning, and operation of institutions of higher education. Publication policy is set by its Publications Committee.

For information about the Association for Institutional Research, write to the following address:

AIR Executive Office
114 Stone Building
Florida State University
Tallahassee, FL 32306-3038

(904) 644-4470

air@mailer.fsu.edu
www.fsu.edu/~air/home.htm

CONTENTS

This volume is a guide for institutional managers who are attempting to leverage the forces of transformation on their campuses. It is not a cookbook but a guidebook of principles and practices for reaping the opportunities and benefits of Knowledge Age learning and prevailing in the face of fiercer competition.

Leveraging the Forces of Transformation on Campus

Donald M. Norris, James L. Morrison

In *Transforming Higher Education: A Vision for Learning in the 21st Century,* Dolence and Norris (1995) provided a framework for viewing the opportunities available to higher learning through total realignment to the needs of Information Age learners. But the metaphor of an "information age" is inadequate. We are virtually awash in information, so much so that each new scrap of information is essentially valueless. We are on the threshold of a Knowledge Age that will be the Age of Learners. Those who align their campuses most effectively to this new age will reap substantial benefits.

The opportunities are vast. Yet these opportunities are not captured by institutions of higher learning that change only marginally. Nor are these opportunities realized if campuses delude themselves into thinking the traditional pace of change will suffice. The spirit of *Transforming Higher Education* was captured in the sentence, "Just because we are changing a great deal does not mean we are transforming." *Transforming Higher Education* was intended to stimulate vision and provoke dialogues on what transformation means on each campus.

Traditional learning will not disappear in the Knowledge Age. However, it will be changed. Every campus will alter its approaches to each facet of scholarship: discovery research, synthesis, teaching, and improvement of practice. Not every campus will attempt to truly "transform" itself, or attempt to be among the leaders in preparing for Knowledge Age learners. But we have discovered many campuses that are reshaping their visions of the future and their capacity to reach new learners or reach old learners in new ways. They are learning how to leverage their transformative efforts. Most campuses can benefit from their insights.

Improving Campus Planning Processes

Transforming Higher Education identified several shortcomings of existing planning processes that prevent them from being truly transformative:

- There is too much planning and too little strategic thinking.
- Existing structures and processes are built for a slower pace of change.
- Academic program development is not linked to institutional strategic thinking.
- Resource allocations are not guided by strategic thinking.
- Planning cycles are expenditure-based.

Campuses should deploy strategic planning guided by transformative vision. This requires that we put the *strategic* back in planning, that we fashion new approaches to campus change.

New Breed of Campus Planning and Change

Planning for the Knowledge Age needs to be more iconoclastic, individualistic, and inclusive. Creating new visions of alternative, assured migration paths to the future is a perpetual process, one creating a number of specific imperatives.

Establish Transformative Expectations—Not Revolution. Higher learning cannot be radically refocused overnight, nor should it be. There are many possible scenarios for the future and a variety of migration paths to those futures. Many of the needed tools for transformation haven't even been invented yet. But even though we may need to change incrementally until our vision is clearer and new tools are available, our actions should be guided by transformative intentions. We need to develop infrastructures and competencies that enable us to move more decisively when opportunities present themselves.

Raise Everyone's Knowledge Base Regarding the Reasons for Undertaking Transformational Initiatives. Campus leadership should engage a broad cross section of the campus community in developing shared visions for the future. Vision is not something that the president, provost, or other leaders foist on the campus. At some level, every campus should convene a colloquium on the opportunities for higher learning and the threat that clinging to old ways poses for their institution. The needs of learners in the Knowledge Age should be essential topics of campus discussion. Consciousness raising should touch faculty, administrators, students, and other stakeholders.

Formalize Inclusive Planning Processes. Planning for the Knowledge Age should involve a diagonal cross section of the campus community. Strategic thinking should welcome ideas and insights on strategy from throughout the campus community. Sometimes the best insights come from some of the youngest participants. Such planning should be continual, even perpetual. It cannot be seen as an exercise on which campuses embark every few years.

Align Resources with Strategies. Some campuses are frozen in amber by the resource commitments made to maintain the existing paradigm. Reallocated resources are needed to nurture transformed initiatives. Realignment of resources to support transformative initiatives, and investment of new resources in information technology and learning technologies and applications, will characterize successful campuses in the Knowledge Age.

Redirect Existing Processes to Transformative Ends. The greatest potential for transformation can be achieved by redirecting existing campus processes, driven by a vision of the infrastructures and competencies needed to serve Knowledge Age learners. The result (though not a radical course change) is a 10–15 degree adjustment in direction, a greater sense of urgency, and increased allocation of resources to transformative initiatives, all of which can propel a campus toward transformation. Existing processes that can be transformed are:

- Strategic thinking and visioning
- Facilities planning
- Academic program planning
- Strategic enrollment management
- Information technology (IT) infrastructure development
- Resource allocation

In addition, campuses need to do a much better job of revenue planning. A new financial paradigm must be discovered for information technology in higher learning, one that treats IT infrastructure as an investment and enables institutions to generate new revenue streams to pay for a high level of IT investment in the future. Investment pools should be created to support the development of Knowledge Age skills.

Launch New Learning Initiatives, Craft New Strategic Alliances. Many of the new learning initiatives for Knowledge Age learners require colleges and universities to form strategic alliances with other institutions, new learning providers and intermediaries, and technology companies. The current flood of virtual university and virtual community college initiatives, most of them involving new strategic alliances, suggests the potential of these opportunities.

Utilize Leverage Points for Change. The ongoing patterns and cadences of campus life provide dozens of leverage points for fostering change. Some are natural events in academic life, while others reflect external interventions:

- Campus strategic planning processes, visioning exercises, environmental scanning, leadership retreats, and campus colloquia on key issues
- Use of external consultants
- Realignment of continuing education or extended education
- Design and construction of new facilities
- Accreditation and academic program review
- Implementation of new information systems or development of new IT infrastructure
- Use of advisory committees for colleges and particular academic programs
- Initiation of continuous quality improvement (CQI) or reengineering programs

- Teaching and learning roundtables
- Reviews of faculty roles and rewards
- New learning initiatives and strategic alliances with other learning providers and intermediaries and technology or edutainment companies
- Review and realignment of troubled programs

The best approach is to combine two or three leverage points to create a new or redirected initiative with greater impact. The case studies in this volume illustrate the power enjoyed by campuses that utilize multiple leverage points.

Communicate Models of Success. The fact of success is not enough. Successes must be chronicled. Too often, campus leadership fails to appreciate the symbolic value of new visions, redirected processes, and case studies found on their campus (or examples from other campuses) that can have high demonstrative value. Individuals from transforming campuses are forming networks to engage in the reflective practice of transformation.

Support Agents of Transformation; Convert Skeptics. To be sure, it is important to "water where the grass is green" and support champions of Knowledge Age scholarship. These champions should win funding for their initiatives and projects. However, it is also necessary to confront skeptics and defenders of the status quo and to challenge the easy assumption that campuses can change marginally and still retain their cachet in the Knowledge Age. The dialogue to win over skeptics and challenge those who feel they can take a bye on the Knowledge Age is critical for every campus. The "pro" side of the debate should be waged not just by campus leadership but by faculty, academic support staff, and others who are employing the tools of Knowledge Age scholarship.

Focus on Strategic Decisions That Facilitate Transformation. Campuses move forward toward the Knowledge Age through decisions, not just plans or strategies. Today's decisions determine whether campuses establish strategic position, information technology and learning infrastructure, and core competencies to take advantage of opportunities over the next five to ten years.

A model for campus transformation should differ from the traditional model of campus change, that is, incremental, slow-to-act (or react), conserving of both the form and essence of tradition, utilizing six-month to two-year projects, and acting sequentially on one or two initiatives at a time. Our future model of transformative change is one in which the campus:

- Uses a five-to-ten-year process or even longer
- Uses multiple vectors of change operating in parallel, not sequentially
- Recognizes that there is no single starting point or ending point for change processes
- Recognizes that future visions of learning should incorporate alternative scenarios and prepare the campus for success under any of them
- Involves broad cross sections of the campus community in strategy setting
- Creates new organizational cultures and then replicates the cultural DNA to other parts of the organization

- Develops Knowledge Age competencies in rapid program development and deployment, new approaches to learning, customer orientation, mass customization (tailoring learning to meet the needs of any individual), supercharged strategic alliances, and generation of new pools of resources

The case studies in this volume either demonstrate how to implement campus transformation or illustrate what can happen if transformation is approached properly.

Outtakes on the Road to Transformation

Many campuses have stumbled in their efforts to introduce the notion of "transformation" to their institution. Or they have dealt with problems using a band-aid approach when fundamental realignment was called for. Often these initiatives have failed by trumpeting the "T" word—transformation—without engaging the faculty and other key elements of the community in understanding what it means. Or they have tried to change by fiat. Some campuses have stumbled by reengineering or restructuring without realigning the institution's vision and culture to new opportunities. Several examples illustrate these outtakes on the road to transformation (their identities have been purposely masked):

The president of a regional state university in the Midwest announced the establishment of a "learning university" initiative with great fanfare, but without buy-in by or understanding on the part of faculty leadership. The initiatives languished for several years before being forgotten.

The leadership of a strategic planning process at a major research university in the West labeled their planning as transformative. This declaration mobilized faculty opposition that stalled the process in its tracks. A vital opportunity was lost.

A private university in the South undertook an extensive restructuring program to overcome a substantial structural deficit. It did not realign its programs, nor did it provide for changing the culture and processes that had led to the deficit. Within a year and a half, the deficit had reemerged.

A private college on the West Coast launched a strategic planning process. When the provost became aware of the potentially transformative implications of the process, he pulled the plug on the venture.

An innovative public university program in the Southwest hired faculty who were in tune with the new culture of the campus. But they hired administrative support staff from existing public institutions without discussing the values of the new program. Within a year, major problems developed.

Most campuses rebound from such missteps, but it takes time. Successful campuses cannot afford to squander time in their preparation for Knowledge Age learning.

New Perspectives on Transformation

The dialogue on transformation of higher education has accelerated dramatically since the publication of *Transforming Higher Education*. Recent works have focused on the big role of IT leadership in transformation (Norris and Dolence, 1996), the emergence of perpetual learning as a metaphor for learning in the Knowledge Age (Norris, 1996), and the development of core competencies for Knowledge Age learning (Norris and Olson, 1997). We have incorporated these new perspectives into our final analysis of what we have learned from the case studies.

Because of the rapid rate of change in these campuses, we have referenced campus Web sites as sources of continually updated insights on these issues. Readers can check the Web sites for new developments at these institutions.

Case Study Examples

We sought case studies that would be useful to a wide range of institutions, from campuses aspiring to achieve fundamental transformation to those wishing to leverage a more limited transformation initiative.

We did not seek campuses that have become Knowledge Age institutions, for two reasons. First, the Knowledge Age is not yet upon us. We are still in the midst of the transition, and most institutions are digitizing their existing services and organizational approaches rather than developing services tailored to Knowledge Age learners. Second, the transition to the Knowledge Age is a five-to-ten-year process, or possibly longer. So we are describing institutions that are in the midst of transformative initiatives. The measure of their success is not having achieved a final end point. Success lies in leveraging the transformation forces on their campus that enable even greater leverage in the future.

References

Dolence, M. G., and Norris, D. M. *Transforming Higher Education: A Vision for Learning in the 21st Century.* Ann Arbor, Mich.: Society for College and University Planning, 1995.

Norris, D. M. "Perpetual Learning as a Revolutionary Creation." *On the Horizon,* Nov.–Dec. 1996, pp. 1–4.

Norris, D. M., and Dolence, M. G. "IT Leadership Is Key to Transformation." *Cause/Effect,* Spring 1996, pp. 12–21.

Norris, D. M., and Olson, M. A. "Preparing for Virtual Commerce in Higher Learning." *Cause/Effect,* Spring 1997, pp. 40–44.

DONALD M. NORRIS is president of Strategic Initiatives, a management consulting firm located in Herndon, Virginia.

JAMES L. MORRISON is professor of educational leadership at the University of North Carolina at Chapel Hill.

*The University of Texas at San Antonio uses its planning for
a new Knowledge Age campus and new facilities on the existing
campus to create a climate for learning in the Knowledge Age.*

Creating a Learning Vision
for the Knowledge Age:
The University of Texas at San Antonio

Donald M. Norris

The University of Texas at San Antonio illustrates how an institution can
launch, redirect, and leverage several change initiatives in parallel to substantially position the university for success in the Knowledge Age. The case
demonstrates the importance of leadership and of leveraging new resources
and opportunities for growth. It also suggests the importance of reshaping the
institution's culture and approach to change.

Of the forces for change, this case illustrates:

- Vision of a technology-rich downtown campus
- Using campus master planning and resource allocation to redirect existing
  processes
- Building IT (information technology) and learning infrastructure
- Creating a Web-based vision of learning to support campuswide dialogue
- Changing the institutional culture for IT and technology-supported learning

These initiatives are creating the institutional infrastructure and context
in which departmental-based change processes can occur.

Institutional History and the Symbolism of
the New Downtown Campus

The University of Texas at San Antonio (UTSA) is a comprehensive university
that is one of the academic campuses of the University of Texas system. Its
main campus is located in the northwest suburbs of San Antonio, a metropolitan area of over one million people; most of the students are commuters.

New Directions for Institutional Research, no. 94, Summer 1997 © Jossey-Bass Publishers

UTSA has grown dramatically over the past twenty years. The university also operates a downtown learning center, called the Downtown Campus, in the Cypress Tower and an extensive distance learning operation.

Through the vision and aggressive action of civic and university leaders, UTSA acquired a parcel of land for the new Downtown Campus. The twelve–acre site is located near both the downtown business district and the barrio, where many of San Antonio's least affluent citizens live. UTSA has never been regarded as closely linked, either physically or philosophically, with these communities. However, the new Downtown Campus is viewed as an important symbol and a mechanism for demonstrating the university's connectedness and commitment to all segments of its community. The master plan for the downtown campus portrayed a high-tech campus having the latest in information technology and modern design. It was conceived to make both architectural and technological statements that the people of this part of San Antonio deserved the very best in learning.

There was another facet to the vision. The Downtown Campus was seen as a mechanism for advancing the use of technology in academic and administrative processes throughout UTSA. New approaches that were launched on the Downtown Campus, and in new facilities for business administration on the main campus, could be used to change the entire university culture over time.

The timing of this vision was fortuitous. The university had been developing its information technology infrastructure aggressively from 1991 to 1995. But the infrastructure was still not ready for prime time, and the level of use by faculty, students, and staff was uneven. New campus facilities at the main campus, the new Downtown Campus, and the accompanying new pools of technological resources would accelerate the adoption of technology at the university.

The Consulting Assignment

The university leadership engaged Strategic Initiatives, Inc., to assess the plans for the Downtown Campus and the university's technology base. There were several key questions:

- Is the basic design concept for the new Downtown Campus sufficiently advanced and forward thinking to position the university for learning in the Knowledge Age?
- Are the planned IT infrastructure and use of IT in learning for the new campus and the entire university sufficiently advanced and flexible for the Knowledge Age?
- What is needed to advance and leverage the use of IT across the entire university?

These questions were addressed through focus groups and discussions with groups of administrators, faculty, staff, and students from the entire university community.

Findings of the Initial Analysis

The initial analysis contained both good news and bad news for the university.

Good Basic Design and Plan for the Downtown Campus. The basic design concept for the Downtown Campus was excellent. From all design perspectives—overall design, symbolism of the campus image, fit with the neighborhood, and flexibility for growth and development—the master plan was excellent. The technology base envisioned for the campus was also on target. The first building would immediately advance the technology envelope of the university and held the capacity to further push that envelope through planned enhancements. Subsequent buildings were already planned that incorporated more advanced technological and learning applications.

The Need for New Administrative and Student Service Vision. The facilities plans were not perfect. The plans for administrative and student support service functions and office facilities were highly traditional. Separate offices for provided for admissions, registration, financial aid, and other functions (for a campus that would start with 1,500–2,000 students). Clearly, greater integration of administrative and student support services and flexible facilities would better serve the needs of the new campus, both initially and over time.

As a result of this recommendation, the university president personally led a design session to reconceptualize the support service functions for the downtown campus and create a more open and flexible facilities plan.

The Need for Integrated Student Service Software. In order to support a customer-focused, integrated approach to student support services, the university needed to upgrade its student and administrative support software. As a result of this recommendation, the university has been pursuing several approaches to the upgrade: acquisition of off-the-shelf software from an existing major provider, creation of Web site-driven solutions, or using products developed by the University of Texas system.

The Centralized IT Mentality and Lack of Academic Involvement in IT Development. During its period of infrastructure development, the university's IT central staff was the only source of expertise and "owned" the infrastructure development process. They operated in a traditional data processing mode, without involving end users in the planning and ownership process. As a result, many academics felt they were not involved in the development process and that IT staff were establishing priorities for academic IT. This placed the central IT staff in an untenable position.

The Need to Enhance Faculty Participation in Knowledge Age Learning. Partly as a result of these forces, faculty at UTSA were slow to adopt the tools of Information Age learning and scholarship. Some colleges were more advanced than others, but the overall level of development was disappointing. Academic leaders were loath to invest resources in technology because they felt the basic system was not under their control.

This basic set of findings spawned immediate and specific actions—as examples, redesign of academic and administrative support space, search for a new administrative software product suite, and fine tuning of some of the technology plans. It also stimulated the president to launch two new initiatives: reshaping the IT organization and infrastructure development, and developing a learning vision for the Knowledge Age. These two initiatives were used to further enhance the change process.

The New Initiative: IT Organization and Infrastructure Development

There were two key components to the IT organization and infrastructure development initiative: a new approach to organization and a new financial paradigm for IT.

A New Organizational Paradigm. The heart of the new organizational model for IT at UTSA was Charles Handy's metaphor of a "shamrock organization." Perfectly suited to IT, this organization consists of three groups of knowledge workers: core competency staff, outsourcing, and temporary staff. Realigning UTSA's conception of IT to this model demonstrated to academic leaders and faculty how they would assume ownership of their part of end user computing. It is being used to rebuild confidence in the direction of academic IT.

Core Competency Staff. UTSA's core competency staff consists of all faculty and staff who use IT to enhance their performance. The size of this group will grow substantially in coming years.

The *core IT staff* are responsible for the inner two layers of the knowledge infrastructure—everything "from the wall back," through networks, computers, and servers (but including some utility functions such as student labs and distance learning)—and for establishing standards for connectivity, maintenance, and training. Central IT staff provide training, or contract for it through outsourcing arrangements, or train the trainers among other IT staff and even end users.

IT associates in administrative and academic units provide troubleshooting, assistance, and training for end users. They need to be proximate to the end users; hence they should be in administrative offices or in the colleges (ultimately, some may even be at lower levels).

One of the key types of specialized IT staff is the *instructional development staff:* IT specialists and pedagogical specialists who assist faculty in infusing technology into their teaching and in creating new, Information Age learningware. These staff are likely to be clustered in faculty laboratory facilities dedicated to such applications. Ultimately, some may be assigned to individual colleges.

As faculty and staff become skillful *end users,* they will spend increasing amounts of time in using IT to enhance their performance. Although they seek assistance from both central IT staff and IT staff in administrative and academic units, end users develop their own capacity to troubleshoot many of their own problems, especially as they relate to homegrown applications.

Outsourcing. UTSA has many outsourcing partners: the DEFINE system at UT Austin, the new student information system software, Internet connection providers for students and faculty, specialized training, and some kinds of troubleshooting and network or equipment maintenance. These will increase over time.

Temporary Staff. Temporary staff are used for installation of equipment and software, specialized training, and new project implementation. Use of temporary staff will also grow in the future.

A New Financial Paradigm for IT. UTSA's greatest resource challenge was to raise sufficient resources to develop and operate an Information Age knowledge infrastructure. It had largely relied on the resource pools associated with the new business building and the Downtown Campus to provide this base. Fundraising was used to bring these pools up to substantial levels, in order to sufficiently outfit the buildings from the start. Much of this equipment will need to be upgraded within three years.

To generate the strategic resources necessary for development and operation of the knowledge infrastructure, the leadership of UTSA is considering and pursuing the following options:

- State formula funding and appropriations. The state of Texas should be pressed to reflect the greater cost of knowledge infrastructure development in funding formulas.
- State initiatives. Aggressively seek TIFF funds, especially for collaborative, cross-sector ventures.
- UT system-funded initiatives and special projects. The ongoing Information Technology Initiative being conducted by the UT system provides UTSA with the opportunity to come forward with some leading-edge projects or special initiatives that may be funded.
- Institutional advancement and capital development. The new idea in institutional advancement is to create funding opportunities attractive to donors who have profited from the technology industries or are intrigued by the potential of Information Age learning. Such opportunities raise the total amount of funding dramatically and direct the money to IT infrastructure.
- Student computing fees and end user fees. Students will have to pay for a greater proportion of the cost of IT services, especially as we get into online delivery and Web site-based learning.
- Foundation and vendor funding for learning initiatives. Independently from capital campaigning, UTSA can pitch to vendors and foundations to support creative learning initiatives. This is important to provide support and incentives for faculty to try new approaches.
- New revenue streams. As UTSA develops the capacity for Information Age commerce, new revenue streams could develop. For example, UTSA could establish a print-on-demand utility for the entire San Antonio area, serving not just UTSA but other colleges, K–12 schools, and local businesses.

UTSA's leadership is pursuing establishment of the shamrock organizational model and creation of a new financial paradigm for IT. These two accomplishments are considered essential to building both the IT infrastructure and the engagement of academics necessary for Knowledge Age learning.

A number of immediate actions were taken. The search for a new CIO was launched. Evaluation of a new student service software suite was undertaken. (Because of uncertainties in the development of new software products, UTSA decided to utilize Web-enhanced versions of existing systems until new products are available.) A new type of support worker, IT support staff, was created for assignment to the new divisions. The organizational structure of academic technology training was rationalized. Temporary staff and outsourcing were used to solve training and software installation problems that developed. A help-desk service was introduced to improve customer service from the IT staff. And an academic advisory group was structured to recommend academic technology innovation and application.

The impact of these actions will be monitored and incorporated in a new strategic planning process dealing with the campus investment in IT.

A New Initiative: Developing a Learning Vision for the Knowledge Age

A second initiative was also recommended: develop a learning vision for UTSA in the Knowledge Age, to be used as the basis for building the IT infrastructure and other learning applications. This mechanism would reiterate the fact that academic insight was driving the development of IT infrastructure.

A Diverse Group, Academic-Driven and with Multiple Constituents. To develop this vision, the president appointed a diverse group that included faculty, administrative staff, and other stakeholders. The group had a predominantly academic flavor. Focus group sessions were held with a wide variety of groups: faculty, administrative staff, students, and external stakeholders.

A Web Site to Capture the Vision, Strategies, and Plans. In order to chronicle the emerging academic vision and make it available to the university community, the Learning Vision Planning Group (LVPG) developed a Web site (http://nmlab.utsa.edu/visions/) to serve as their "canvas." This device helped both in capturing the work in progress and in soliciting input on particular ideas, visions, and strategies. Structuring the Web site also forced the LVPG to think through an important issue: "How do we communicate the challenges of moving the campus forward to embrace learning in the Knowledge Age?"

Rapid Prototyping of a Vision for Ongoing Commitment and Revision. The traditional academic approach to creating a vision for the future is to discuss the elements of the vision in great detail, considering all possibilities and complexities, and then assemble the elements of the future into a whole. This is like trying to design an elephant by committee: crafting each piece in detail, assembling the pieces into a whole, and finding that the committee has created a camel!

UTSA created its future vision and scenarios by first spending time talking about the elements of the future and the aspirations of the participants, and then creating several alternative future visions and debating the merits of the alternatives. This is called rapid prototyping. It is a way of creating consistent, compelling future scenarios and visions. These alternatives reinforce the point that there is not one future but many possible futures. The winning institutional planning process positions the college or university to be successful under any likely future scenario.

The UTSA planning group created a rapid prototype vision of the university in the Knowledge Age. That much was easy. But all the faculty members on the committee lamented that they couldn't even think about how to move forward toward that vision because they were held prisoner by today's paradigms, processes of evaluation, and conventions. To articulate this concern, the committee addressed the issue of identifying and overcoming the barriers to achieving a Knowledge Age vision for the university, and how to surmount that opposition.

Rip Back to the Present to Identify Barriers, Corrective Actions, and Measures of Success. The committee used the future vision to illuminate the barriers that prevented faculty from engaging in innovation and moving out toward the future. The key ingredient was time, or lack of it; faculty were fully "booked" under their existing responsibilities. Most models of innovation call for the faculty to personally invest sweat equity to develop IT-based approaches to teaching and learning. So the LVPG chronicled these barriers but then went on to suggest how the university could launch processes to overcome them. Further, they suggested both short-term and long-term measures of success under a heading on the Web site: "How Will We Know We Are Succeeding?"

The following descriptions summarize the key items regarding barriers, corrective actions, and measures of success. By accessing the Web site, readers can review the full details and how they were presented to the campus community for discussion.

Barriers to Innovation. The barriers to innovation included a familiar litany of academic issues:

- Existing faculty evaluation criteria not recognizing many types of innovation
- University's emphasis on research rather than learning innovation
- Low level of faculty skills in application of technology to learning
- Limited training to enhance those skills
- Inadequate seed money for release time and support of innovation
- Lack of models and mechanisms for sharing ideas on innovation
- Inadequate resources for infusion of technology into teaching and learning

Actions to Overcome Barriers. The LVPG suggested that individual and department-based innovation could proceed with greater vigor if the university changed both the incentive structure and resources available. Their recommendations:

- Change faculty evaluation criteria to recognize IT-based innovation in the promotion and tenure process.
- Examine the evaluation criteria to ensure that teaching is being adequately rewarded.
- Expand mechanisms for faculty training and professional development in the use of IT tools to support learning.
- Provide a variety of means of faculty development, including individual mentoring by students—in the privacy of faculty offices—on use of IT tools.
- Introduce faculty to use of instructional development teams, including senior faculty, instructional development staff, and students, so as to leverage faculty time.
- Provide competitive pools of resources for faculty development and instructional development.
- Develop new sources of revenue for IT-based innovation and for creation of leveraging.
- Change the resource paradigm for IT to infuse new funding into IT use by end users, at the departmental level.

These actions are described in greater detail on the Web site.

Measures of Success. The LVPG suggested both short-term and long-term measures of success that would demonstrate how well the university is faring in addressing these issues. These measures can also be found on the Web site under the section "How Will We Know We Are Succeeding?"

Best Practices. The Web site also provided a mechanism for showcasing best practices and innovative applications developed by UTSA faculty. These were used to illustrate how to leverage existing resources to create IT-based innovation.

Invite Campuswide Comment Via Web Site. The Web site provided a mechanism that can be used in the future for campus response to the learning vision and its implications. In the fullness of time, this can be utilized to engage the campus community in dialogue on the emergence of new approaches to learning in the Knowledge Age. It provides a touchstone against which the various learning initiatives, IT infrastructure development initiatives, and plans for new buildings and the downtown campus can be gauged.

Next Steps. UTSA is moving forward in parallel with several initiatives that have been redirected:

- Downtown Campus planning and construction
- Construction of new buildings at the main campus
- Development of IT infrastructure and the new IT culture
- Strategic enrollment management, using an enrollment management consultant
- Faculty development of Knowledge Age tools
- Distance Learning initiative

These initiatives continue to be leveraged and have resulted in decisions that are reshaping the university's direction.

As the university moves forward with its plans for development, the learning vision and related discussion provide a useful dimension to the dialogue. Universities must find ways to elevate the thinking of all members of the campus community about the opportunities and challenges for learning in the Knowledge Age. Mechanisms such as those employed by UTSA must be found to engage broad cross sections of faculty, staff, students, and other stakeholders in exploring how learning will change.

For more information on the University of Texas at San Antonio, visit their Web site (http://www.utsa.edu). There you will find links offering an overview of UTSA and the community it serves as well as information on admissions, student affairs, and UTSA outreach programs.

For an in-depth discussion and mission statement on the learning vision and UTSA's efforts to capitalize on the opportunities for Information Age learning, follow the link from their home page to the Learning Vision Project.

DONALD M. NORRIS *is president of Strategic Initiatives, a management consulting firm located in Herndon, Virginia.*

Lincoln University uses its Futures Program as a powerful tool of transformation to position the university to confront major changes in New Zealand's educational environment.

Using the Futures Program as a Tool for Transformation: Lincoln University, New Zealand

James L. Morrison, Allan Sargison, Debra Francis

This chapter describes the Lincoln Futures Program and how anticipatory management tools were used to support the transformation of Lincoln's organizational culture. We conclude by describing the value of this approach in developing strategies to meet the challenges of the twenty-first century.

Over the past decade, Lincoln University, in Christchurch, New Zealand, has grown from being a college of Canterbury University with much of its teaching focused on agricultural science to become a full university offering a broad range of programs with a particular focus on natural resources and commerce. As such, it is the smallest university in New Zealand, having 3,900 full-time students and 450 faculty and staff members.

Of the familiar forces of transformation, this case represents use of visioning and strategy setting, campuswide dialogue and vision, redirecting campus planning processes, and launching the transformation of campus culture. These initiatives are positioning Lincoln University to deal with a dramatically and continuously changing educational environment in New Zealand and the entire Australasian region.

Change Comes to Lincoln University

Until six years ago, Lincoln had all the characteristics of a traditional university: a comparatively well funded collegiate culture with hands-off management and complex committee structures, and characterized by slow decision making and resistance to change.

In the 1990s, reduced government funding and the opening of the higher education market to polytechnics triggered the development of a more commercial approach to management. This included a more businesslike management structure with defined accountabilities, accrual accounting based on cost and profit centers, a relatively comprehensive management information system (MIS), developing subsidiary for-profit companies to conduct applied research for commercial firms, a research-based marketing program, emphasis on strategic planning with a ten-year horizon, performance assessment, and a large investment in information technology (IT) for teaching and management. A major problem faced the administration and faculty: how to galvanize the core academic culture of the university to realign to meet the challenges lying ahead.

Overview of the Lincoln Futures Program

The Lincoln Futures Program was designed to use several anticipatory management tools described by Ashley and Morrison (1995). These tools encourage widespread use of organizational stakeholders to anticipate changes in the external environment and to link these anticipated changes to internal decision making. The underlying assumption for Lincoln was that by harnessing the intellectual power of stakeholders to (1) identify signals of change, (2) analyze the implications of these signals for the university, and (3) design actions in light of these implications, not only would the university be able to design and implement creative plans but these plans would have the active support of the majority of stakeholders. In effect, this would transform the organizational culture.

Establishing and Staffing the Program

The Lincoln Futures Program was established in mid–1995 by way of employing a full-time futures analyst to coordinate the program and to work with the vice-chancellor (whose U.S. counterpart would be the chancellor or president) and the registrar (U.S. counterpart the executive vice president) in implementing the program. A staff newsletter expressed the goals of the futures program:

- To stimulate discussion between Lincoln University staff and other stakeholders about the university's best possible/most appropriate future directions
- To help develop a shared sense of Lincoln's future direction and core activities within its staff
- To anticipate and prepare for potential threats to Lincoln University from the environment outside the university
- To be as creative as possible about Lincoln's future teaching, research, and entrepreneurial directions
- To position Lincoln University strategically with regard to future markets for our services
- To be proactive and cutting edge as a university

Using Consultation

An outside consultant was employed to facilitate the initial anticipatory management workshop, which included all council members (the university's governing board, whose chair is titled chancellor), senior administrators, and selected faculty and staff members. This workshop focused on the tools of environmental scanning, vulnerability assessments, and issues management. The design and results of that workshop were replicated by the futures analyst with various groups throughout the university over a fifteen-month period. In addition, the futures analyst developed and coordinated a comprehensive and systematic environmental scanning process that included some eighty faculty, staff, and students. At the conclusion of the period under review (May 1995–August 1996), the outside consultant facilitated two successive workshops on scenario planning that incorporated the products of the scanning, vulnerability assessments, and issues management processes to flesh out possible alternative futures and to derive creative strategic options for the university to pursue in the corporate[1] (five–year) plan. Throughout this period, university faculty and staff members participated in a number of these activities, in the variety of ways described below.

The Transformation Tools Used by the Futures Program

The Futures Program deployed four transformation tools: (1) environmental scanning, (2) issue management, (3) vulnerability assessments, and (4) scenario-based planning.

Environmental Scanning. Environmental scanning entails actively seeking signals of change in the social, technological, economic, environmental, and political sectors of the external environment. The external environment consists of the market environment, the industry environment, and the macroenvironment. Scanning the market environment, for example, involves seeking signals of change in the demographics of students served by the institution. Scanning the industry environment involves looking for signals of change in how other educational providers are serving their clientele. Scanning the macroenvironment includes seeking signs of change—from local to global—that could affect the future of the organization.

We began the Lincoln futures program with an introductory presentation on major drivers of change that could affect colleges and universities in the twenty-first century. The presentation was followed by a daylong workshop with Lincoln's council, senior staff, and selected faculty members, where, in small groups, they identified key emerging trends and potential events that could affect the future of Lincoln. We also conducted several exercises following the outline described by Morrison (1992) in which participants prioritized the trends and events, conducted several elementary analyses on the implications of the most critical ones, and drafted recommendations as to what actions Lincoln should take, given the analysis. The intent was to introduce the concept and process of scanning in a workshop format so that participants would experience the process and willingly agree to participate in this aspect of the Lincoln futures program.

The scanning workshop was well received; some eighty faculty, students, and staff members agreed to review assigned information sources and send the futures analyst either abstracts or full copy of items they found worth attention. The futures analyst in turn summarized these items and distributed the summaries with key questions to various constituencies within the Lincoln community. For an excerpt, see their Web site:

http://sunsite.unc.edu/horizon/welcome/exhibits/exhibit1.html.

The intent was to focus the attention of Lincoln University stakeholders on developments in the external world and raise questions vis-à-vis their implications for the future direction of the university.

Issues Management. Issues management is a structured process to identify emerging issues that the university must address in organizational planning. The general concept is that the scanning committee identifies salient issues through the use of issues analysis worksheets and develops issue briefs on those most salient for use by the vice-chancellor's Futures Group (VCFG), as illustrated in Figure 3.1.

For an example of an analysis worksheet, see their Web site:

http://sunsite.unc.edu/horizon/welcome/exhibits/exhibit2.html

The Futures Group committee members range from senior administrators through academic program directors and scanning and focus group conveners. They review the issues briefs, prioritize them, and assign selected issues for inclusion in the corporate planning system, the issues management system, or the strategic scenarios group. For examples of such assignments, see their Web site:

http://sunsite.unc.edu/horizon/welcome/exhibits/exhibit3.html

VCFG decisions are described in futures newsletters and discussion papers distributed throughout the university community.

Vulnerability Assessments. Vulnerability assessments are designed to identify the organizational supports that underpin the university's successful functioning, analyze the threats to which these supports are vulnerable, and outline anticipatory responses to these threats (Morrison and Keller, 1992–93). This is another approach to stimulating the development of flexible strategies to deal with expected and unexpected events or trends in the institution's external environment. At Lincoln, we conducted the vulnerability assessment through a workshop format using council members, faculty members, and key members of the university staff.

The assessment proceeds in four steps.

Step 1: Specify critical supports on which the organization depends, and then identify specific organizational strengths. Strengths are viewed from the perspective of how well the institution addresses these supports. Further steps focus

Figure 3.1. Strategic Futures Analysis at Lincoln University

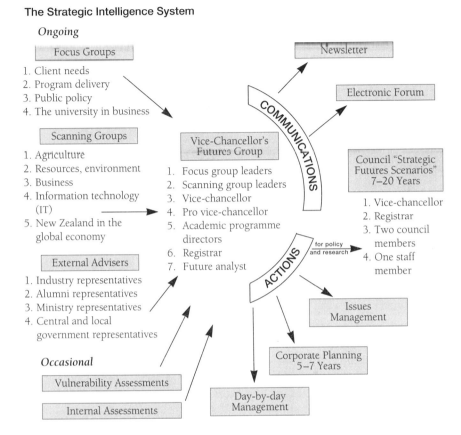

The Strategic Intelligence System

Ongoing

Focus Groups
1. Client needs
2. Program delivery
3. Public policy
4. The university in business

Scanning Groups
1. Agriculture
2. Resources, environment
3. Business
4. Information technology (IT)
5. New Zealand in the global economy

External Advisers
1. Industry representatives
2. Alumni representatives
3. Ministry representatives
4. Central and local government representatives

Occasional

Vulnerability Assessments

Internal Assessments

COMMUNICATIONS

Vice-Chancellor's Futures Group
1. Focus group leaders
2. Scanning group leaders
3. Vice-chancellor
4. Pro vice-chancellor
5. Academic programme directors
6. Registrar
7. Future analyst

ACTIONS

for policy and research

Newsletter

Electronic Forum

Council "Strategic Futures Scenarios" 7–20 Years
1. Vice-chancellor
2. Registrar
3. Two council members
4. One staff member

Issues Management

Corporate Planning 5–7 Years

Day-by-day Management

on those forces, conditions, trends, and events that could damage organizational supports. Note that a support can be tangible (for example, a physical resource) or intangible (legislation, or social values that make a service or product desirable).

Supports were specified in such categories as needs and wants served by the organization that underpin the demand for its products and services, resources and assets, stability of costs relative to competition, and technologies. For example, in the category of needs and wants served by the institution, society needs graduates who are computer literate as well as computer systems analysts. Many academic programs across Lincoln have modified their curricula in order to train graduates to work effectively in an interdependent global society based upon information technology. The workshop participants identified certain strengths of Lincoln in this area, including educating the workforce, conducting basic research, preserving and disseminating knowledge, providing leadership to society, and focusing on students' skill development.

Step 2: Identify the vulnerabilities to which each support category is exposed. In this step, workshop groups proceed through their responses to the categories in step 1, but this time target vulnerabilities or threats are expressed as events, trends, or issues. That is, the groups use the ideas developed as strengths in step 1 to ask questions about what could occur in the external environment to affect these strengths. For example, for the first category, needs and wants served, relevant vulnerability questions are whether a need or want could be served in some other way by some other institution; whether the need for a product or service could disappear; and if so, under what circumstances.

Lincoln's vulnerabilities identified in response to these questions, stated as potential events, included corporations' becoming educators of choice, Lincoln's inflexibility to a changing marketplace, and the public's loss of trust in Lincoln's ability to deliver, to name just a few.

Step 3: Analyze key vulnerabilities. After using the first two steps to identify a rough description of vulnerabilities, the council members, managers, academics, and general staff members refined the descriptions into the following sets of key threats facing Lincoln:

- Public policy changes in an MMP environment, particularly those relating to funding, governance, and ownership of higher education
- Increasing competition from international education providers (as through distance delivery or franchise) and from noncredentialed, nontraditional, or noninstitutional providers
- Increasingly diverse and demanding clients
- Increasing complexity of knowledge and need for high-risk decisions amid uncertainty, at both corporate and business-unit levels
- Changes in stakeholders' perceptions of universities
- Increasing requirements to utilize technology and a variety of delivery modes in order to achieve efficiencies, respond to diverse learning needs, and access markets

Lincoln's specific vulnerabilities include its small size, distance from a population center, inflexible human resource management, and lack of management capacity for product development.

Step 4: Identify anticipatory actions and assign responsibility for these actions. The next step after agreeing upon the vulnerabilities of the institution was to develop recommendations, decide what actions were needed, and assign responsibility and time lines for each action. For an example of such recommendations after the vulnerability audit, see their Web site:

http://sunsite.unc.edu/horizon/welcome/exhibits/exhibit4.html

Scenario-Based Planning. The inputs and experience gained from the environmental scanning process, issues management process, and vulnerability audits around campus served as feedstock for the last tool we used: scenario planning.

Scenarios are comprehensive, internally consistent, long-term perspectives on the future. They serve as a framework for strategic thinking, providing insightful understanding of the dynamics of change and a fuller consideration of the range of opportunities and threats facing the organization, thereby reducing the organization's vulnerability to surprises. Scenarios encourage an expanded range of strategy options; more resilient, flexible strategy; and better assessment of risks. They also provide a sound basis for continuous monitoring of the institution's environment and a common framework for our thinking about the future.

A small team of senior administrators and selected faculty members spent four days in the initial scenario development process. This team was supplemented by council members who helped "scrub" the scenarios and develop strategic options to be included in the corporate plan. We used the six-step process originally developed by SRI International as modified into a five-step process by Morrison and Wilson (1996; 1997).

Step 1: Frame the decision focus. This step has two objectives: determine which decision(s) the scenarios should be designed to illuminate, and identify issues involved in the decision.

Workshop participants determined that for Lincoln the decision focus involved answering the question: What will Lincoln University be doing in ten years? Several key elements revolved around the decision focus:

- Who will be Lincoln's primary clients—society, government, staff, students, industry—and what are their expectations?
- What is Lincoln's "corporate" strategy?
- What is Lincoln's "business" strategy?

Step 2: Identify the key decision factors (KDFs). KDFs are "things we would like to know about the future when we make the decision." The key decision factors identified by workshop participants included (1) how and by what mechanisms universities and students will be funded by government, (2) what the demographic trends are, and (3) what the future of computer technology is.

Step 3: Assess environmental forces. Which forces, trends, and events will most help in shaping the future course of the KDFs? Workshop participants determined the following to be underlying forces:

- World population growth and limited land area
- IT and communication technology
- Repositioning of universities in postindustrial society
- Individual choice and client orientation
- New Zealand's economy and global economy
- Complexity of knowledge
- Pacific Rim geopolitical development

The trends that result from these environmental forces include changing social and global attitudes toward education, technology, and the environment.

The advancement of university technology, the changing infrastructure of Pacific Rim education, and future agreements between telecommunications companies in the Pacific and in North America are all events that will shape the future of the KDFs affecting Lincoln University.

Step 4: Determine scenario logics. In this step, we first identified the critical "axes of uncertainty" and then defined the logical extremes of each axis. Scenario logics are differing theories about the way the world might work. From the logics available, the scenarios to be elaborated were selected on the criteria that the total group needed to be different, plausible, internally consistent, and useful for decision making. Using these criteria, the logics considered for scenario production included:

Environment
Power sharing
Provision for and relevance of higher education
Global economy and the economic well-being of New Zealand
Government size
Dominating values
Pacific Rim stability
World population growth impact on New Zealand
Wars

Step 5: Elaborate scenarios. Scenario writers used the "ends" of three logics to elaborate scenarios. For example, one of the scenarios was titled "Sustainable political correctness." This scenario, which may be found at:

http://sunsite.unc.edu/horizon/welcome/exhibits/exhibit5.html

was based on biculturalism in New Zealand, sustainable practice in global environmental management, and a high-growth New Zealand economy. The logic of scenario analysis is that there are critical axes of uncertainty; the future will be different depending upon which axis develops. The purpose of the analysis is to describe alternative, plausible, and structurally different views of the future so that we can confront and structure the spectrum of planning uncertainty in a usable manner, identify the full range of opportunities and threats likely to confront the institution, and use scenarios as test beds for assessing the resilience and payoff of alternative strategy and resource allocation options. In order to use scenario planning as a transformation tool, we involved a number of stakeholders from across the institution to analyze and develop strategic options for consideration in the corporate plan. The results of this process are summarized next, in the overall context of the Lincoln Futures program.

The Lincoln Futures Program in Operation

The futures program was developed as a mechanism for merging the outputs from the application of different transformational tools and was designed to coordinate with existing planning processes. It was based on the activities of scanning and focus groups, as illustrated in Figure 3.1. The groups of faculty, staff, and students were organized around mission-critical disciplinary and process areas of the university's operation. Each had a convener and a number of external advisers located in business or in government. They posted their insights about future trends, issues, or problems to a Web site on the university's Intranet called "Environmental Scanning." Contributions varied from aphoristic one-liners to detailed analytical theses, some of which were circulated in print versions. Within three months of commencing their activities, these groups had posted some three hundred items to the Web site. Group members were located at all levels in the organizational hierarchy; they were asked to be involved because of their ability to think creatively. Even so, they needed practice before they became comfortable with thinking in the long time horizon required by the futures program.

Any faculty or staff member (or student) was able to view the items posted to the Web site and encouraged to comment on them. Scanning group conveners then sorted these items, correlated them with the results of the vulnerability assessments and internal analyses, and referred them to the vice-chancellor's Futures Group. Scanning group conveners were excited by the opportunity to advocate their response to issue analysis directly to those with the organizational power to implement changes. Although senior managers were sometimes forced to confront issues they would rather have avoided in these meetings, they too valued the process. Issues surfacing from this activity were sent, for example, to an issues management team for the development of a specified action plan. A great deal of material also fell out for inclusion in the corporate or operational plans. Broad or clustered issues were referred to the council's Strategic Scenarios Group for later production of alternative scenarios, which then formed the basis for a review of the existing corporate plan and for development of new strategic options.

Administrators and faculty were kept informed of all of these developments through the Intranet Web site and by means of regular newsletters and discussion papers. The relative priorities assigned to various issues, for example, were posted to the site following each meeting of the vice-chancellor's group.

From Tools to Strategy

Lincoln University's council and senior administrators believe that the tools of transformation used over the past year have provided a set of imperatives for the strategic repositioning of the institution. These are being translated into the university's corporate plan, which has a one-to-five-year time horizon, as well as into longer-range contingency plans.

The scenario production process culminated in a major review of existing strategy and in a workshop exercise to generate new strategic options, which was attended by line and corporate managers and by members of the Lincoln council. In this workshop, nine scenarios were analyzed in small-group format, both vertically in terms of what each implied for new strategic options and horizontally across particular areas of strategic operation. In the latter exercise, groups were formed to discuss Lincoln's processes, products, and financial viability. These general topics were then disaggregated into particular issue areas. Processes, for example, included such issues as outsourcing of services, reengineering of core processes, and product development processes. The product group worked on issues such as the undergraduate-postgraduate mix and franchising, while the financial analysts examined issues such as capital structure, disinvestment, and risk profiling. Each of these issue areas was analyzed against the nine scenarios. These exercises, when collated, generated a set of strategic options that then formed the top layer of Lincoln's corporate plan. To view these specific strategic options, please visit the Web site listed at the end of this chapter for the complete Lincoln University transformation study.

A senior member of the council concluded the last workshop with these words: "To transform we must leverage technology intelligently to improve the quality of our products; exploit the emerging lifelong learning markets; enter into dynamic strategic alliances; rebalance the infrastructure, physical and human, to support necessary investments in innovation and excellence; build strong leadership in Lincoln's core business; be responsive to markets; become market leaders in our core business; and improve program development and other core processes."

The council member stressed that the key strategic positioning question for Lincoln University is: How does a small, niche university which is remote from its markets survive in an increasingly competitive environment? His answer: focus on a few areas of core competency in which Lincoln has sufficient critical mass to be successful by doing its business well. What Lincoln does must be first class; products must be supported by high-value-adding processes. Lincoln can only build on a sound financial base. To remain small Lincoln must use alliances and at all times ensure quality. Therefore, Lincoln's key strategies must be to:

- Enhance the alignment of market demand, strategic positioning, and product mix
- Align research capacity to strategic positioning
- Foster postgraduate programs, with quality experience and supervision
- Develop and manage sustainable strategic relationships to give effect to our strategic positioning
- Use information technology innovatively to gain strategic advantage
- Ensure that people are valued, involved, supported, and developed throughout the organization
- Ensure that the organization is a fun place to work and learn

Overall, the scenario analysis workshop provided for lively and productive debate among governors and managers with regard to strategic positioning. A major redefinition of Lincoln's positioning was agreed upon, which deemphasized the university's earlier "growth at all costs" strategy. The new positioning would lead to a more tightly defined niche positioning on Lincoln's natural resources (core competencies) and a decision to remain small. Lincoln's senior leadership believes that the small size can be hedged by creative use of strategic alliances and joint ventures, particularly those involving the franchise of program products.

Having concluded this exercise, Lincoln's leaders must now promote the revised strategies and maximize buy-in from internal stakeholders. This is a demanding change agency task, one that will be run by academic rather than corporate managers. On the other hand, the futures work on the Lincoln campus over the past year has ensured that the items in the plan are not a surprise to Lincoln's faculty and staff. These stakeholders have been clearly alerted through the scanning process and discussion in vulnerability workshops, issues meetings, and other events. The progress from scanning to eventual strategy has been much more visible and interactive than was formerly the case in Lincoln's corporate planning rounds.

As Lincoln's vice-chancellor, Bruce Ross, stated, "Through the futures program, the information and issues it generates, and the internal debate which flows from it, Lincoln aims to develop a compelling vision for learning in the twenty-first century."

To view the complete Lincoln University transformation study, please visit their Web site:

http://sunsite.unc.edu/horizon/welcome/transforming.html

For more information on the departments and programs at Lincoln University, New Zealand, visit their Internet site (http://www.lincoln.ac.nz). There you will find a complete list of departments and links to Lincoln University's library resources.

Note

1. In a university, *corporate* strategy relates to institutional positioning; *business* strategy relates to divisional positioning.

References

Ashley, W. C., and Morrison, J. L. *Anticipatory Management: 10 Power Tools for Achieving Excellence Into the 21st Century*. Leesburg, Va.: Issue Action Press, 1995.

Morrison, J. L. "Environmental Scanning." In M. A. Whitely, J. D. Porter, and R. H. Fenske (eds.), *A Primer for New Institutional Researchers*. Tallahassee, Fla.: Association for Institutional Research, 1992.

Morrison, J., and Keller, G. "Newest Tool: The Institutional Vulnerability Audit." *Planning for Higher Education*, Winter 1992–93, pp. 21, 27–34.

Morrison, J. L., and Wilson, I. "The Strategic Management Response to the Challenge of Global Change." In H. Didsbury (ed.), *Future Vision, Ideas, Insights, and Strategies*. Bethesda, Md.: World Future Society, 1996.

Morrison, J. L., and Wilson, I. "Analyzing Environments and Developing Scenarios for Uncertain Times." In M. Peterson, D. Dill, and L. Mets (eds.), *Planning and Management for a Changing Environment: A Handbook on Redesigning Postsecondary Education*. San Francisco: Jossey-Bass, 1997.

JAMES L. MORRISON is professor of educational leadership at the University of North Carolina at Chapel Hill.

ALLAN SARGISON is the registrar of Lincoln University, New Zealand.

DEBRA FRANCIS is the futures analyst at Lincoln University, New Zealand.

The University of Calgary has embarked on a major institutional transformation effort as it enters its second thirty years as a research university. This effort is aimed at significant cultural change within the university in order to ensure its prosperity in a rapidly changing environment.

Meaningful Engagement for Sustained Change: The University of Calgary

Howard Yeager, Gayla Rogers, Donna Finley

The University of Calgary illustrates how a campuswide visioning process can be utilized to leverage and unleash the forces of change. This case demonstrates extensive use of campus visioning and strategizing groups, broad participatory visioning processes, redirection of existing planning and resource allocation processes, and opportunities for Knowledge Age Learning.

The University of Calgary, like other Canadian institutions, has been undergoing substantial change and resource reallocation over the past decade. To leverage these efforts, the university embarked on a major institutional transformation initiative.

This initiative began in the spring of 1996, with the purpose of examining the rapidly changing environment for both the university and postsecondary education in general, to learn more about new challenges and opportunities for the university to engage, and to set and implement new strategic directions. The process has been characterized by high levels of consultation and dialogue both on the university campus and in the Calgary community. It has been facilitated by external experts in organizational change, who have guided the process and helped the campus mobilize its expertise to face the many issues that have arisen.

These efforts will result in a series of implemented changes, and the university plans to continue with several cycles of redesign and implementation efforts during the next two or three years.

The University and Its Environment

The University of Calgary is relatively large (twenty-three thousand students) and research intensive ($65 million in outside research funding), with sixteen faculties, including most professional schools. Although only thirty years old, it has grown rapidly along with the city of Calgary, which hosted the 1988 Winter Olympics and is one of two finalist cities to host the World Exposition in 2005.

Calgary has grown into a major technological and business city from its early days as the center for the oil and gas industry's expansion in Western Canada. The university has modern facilities, innovative academic programming, and an entrepreneurial spirit; it reflects many of the best values of the city of Calgary itself.

Mission Statement and the Institutional Development Plan

Upon his arrival in 1988, President Murray Fraser embarked on a process to build upon then-existing institutional plans and generate more widespread understanding of the need for overall institutional planning. This came at a time when the university had developed world-class facilities and stature from its role in the Winter Olympics. A significant first step was the creation and approval of the university's mission statement, which was accomplished in 1990.

The emergence of a strong institutional identity was one feature of this statement, which helped to serve as a basis for planning. This document was crafted to provide a policy framework for development plans for the institution as a whole and for individual academic departments and faculties, as well as providing criteria for their evaluation. The mission statement contained a series of objectives, which were used as chapter titles in the drafting and approval of the institutional development plan in 1991. This plan described the various actions the university was taking to achieve the objectives set out in the mission statement, and it identified further actions it was committed to taking.

Academic Department and Faculty Plans

Next, the planning focus was shifted to individual departments and faculties, which were asked to prepare planning documents with a common format and content. These consisted of a unit self-study, internal and external environmental scans, a vision statement or description of a desired future, and a plan to allocate or reallocate resources to achieve that future. In 1991, the common fiscal assumption for all units was that increases in resources were unlikely, but that assumption was modified and plans were revised in 1992 to assume a 15–20 percent reduction in resources over a five-year period. This shift was reinforced and culminated in a presidential address to the university community in January 1993, when President Fraser announced plans to reduce academic budgets by 17 percent and nonacademic budgets by 20 percent (both on average) over five years. This preceded by one year the announced provincial operating grant reductions.

Institutional Committees and the Integration of Academic and Financial Planning

The board of governors and the general faculties council (GFC) are the two governing bodies of the university. Authority for all financial matters rests with the board, and development of academic and scholarly programs emanates from the GFC. Overcoming a problem that many universities experience, the University of Calgary links academic planning with budgetary decisions through its GFC committee structure. The university planning committee of the GFC is chaired by the president (who is also the chair of the GFC) and contains ex-officio members, several elected faculty members, and two student leaders. This is the senior academic planning committee of the GFC, and it receives input from other GFC committees, most notably the academic program committee, the facilities and services planning committee, and the research policy committee (each of which relates in turn to a vice presidential portfolio). The linkage of this academic planning to budgeting and the board of governors is achieved through the university budget committee (TUBC). TUBC has virtually the same membership as UPC, with certain modifications. The chair is transferred to one of the GFC-elected faculty members, some administrators participate as resource persons, and the chair of the planning and finance committee of the board is an ex-officio member. This committee reports directly to the board, thus effectively linking academic planning with budgeting.

The UPC reviewed the sixty-six individual department plans and sixteen faculty plans in 1991–92 and prepared a list of eight institutional priority objectives from the mission statement to be used as criteria for their assessment. Budgetary decisions for differential funding to faculties were linked to reviews of their revised academic plans in 1992–93 and 1993–94, as were decisions to restore or reallocate vacant academic positions across faculties. The funds that were initially recovered by budget reductions were targeted for reallocation to drive institutional planning. This was accomplished through the creation of a planning initiatives fund, into which faculty funds were collected and then dispersed on the direction of the president and UPC to achieve specific goals. This process thus used internally mandated budget reductions to finance institutional planning objectives with well-announced criteria.

Provincial Budget Reductions and the Access Fund

In January 1994 the Department of Advanced Education and Career Development (AECD) announced a 21 percent reduction to all provincial postsecondary institutions over a three-year period, in a sequence of 11 percent, 7 percent, and 3 percent. It suggested that a 5 percent reduction in compensation to all employees be incorporated into responses to this reduction (which was subsequently agreed to within the university). The existing budget planning was able to respond effectively to these anticipated reductions, although their magnitude severely curtailed the financing of institutional change. As well, AECD announced the creation of a Can. $47 million access fund for all postsecondary institutions, and a competitive process by which these funds would be distributed based on institutions' willingness to create new programs for students with an emphasis on future employability. The goal was to create ten thousand new places for students in the postsecondary system. The three phases of applications for this fund have now been completed, and the University of Calgary has received funding for approximately fifteen hundred new students from this process. This has helped to mitigate the negative effects of the budget cutbacks and has supported innovative academic programming proposals. While academic planning focused on access fund proposals, budgetary planning concentrated on minimizing the negative consequences of rapid budget reductions. Some help was found using several early-retirement incentive plans, starting as early as 1993. The last of the early retirees will leave in 1997.

Current Institutional Planning Activities

During the past two years, additional planning by senior administrators and deans has concentrated on the basic forces that affect the university's environment: shifting student demographics, increasing competition in the postsecondary system, rapid globalization of human activities, limits to public and private support for both learning and research, increased demands for accountability in academic programs (which are linked to fundamental changes in the employment market), and the impact of electronic communications and new information technologies on all activities.

In order to address these issues, the GFC committee structure was first reviewed and streamlined in 1994 to remove barriers to program and policy changes. This review also resulted in creation of a series of task forces to bring together staff and student expertise to address the most urgent of these challenges. These efforts were initiated in September 1995 through the creation of:

- Technology task force: its mandate is to analyze various issues related to the use of electronic communications and information technologies to support university activities, and propose processes and plans to effectively address them. Research into the needs of students and budgetary advice have been among their first activities.
- Globalization task force: this group has developed a plan for rapid internationalization of the university's activities, in terms of the composition of its student body, development of global partners in learning and research, and enrichment of the experiences and skills of its students.
- The learning and instructional development subcommittee: this group concentrates on improvement and enrichment of the learning environment and has engaged in campuswide dialogue to develop a bank of learning resources to support curriculum reform and improved instructional methodologies.

These groups are unlike normal university committees. They were created as competency-based teams to engage in high-priority, institutional-level issues. The teams are composed of faculty, staff, and students, who are recruited for specific expertise, their credibility on campus, and their ability to be active listeners and consensus builders. This composition reflects the strong value the university has placed on inclusivity during these times of stress. For each team, the need to engage faculty, staff, students, alumni, and key business and community leaders is a central part of their mandate. As well, effective and multiple types of communications are encouraged, in order to move beyond the (much-cherished) academic debate mode to collaborative discussions for effective solutions. Each team has developed a sense of urgency about its work and sees itself to be a driver of change.

These teams are not decision-making bodies; they report to the GFC and the board of governors. They have made rapid progress, and their work has been augmented by a fourth team created in the spring of 1996, the coordination task force.

The Coordination Task Force

This group of thirteen faculty, staff, and students was formed to lead the institution during the first phase of the transformation effort. Created as a time-limited team by the university's senior planning committee, it was given two mandates. First the CTF was directed to develop a plan for institutional direction, and refine it through continuous interaction with the university community. Second, it was asked to coordinate existing innovative efforts and identify additional issues and activities that must be addressed so that an integrated institutional approach can emerge. The team members were seconded from other responsibilities on a nearly full-time basis for a period of eight months, with some rotation in membership to ensure full staffing. The team worked together in a single location and utilized modern electronic communications and information technologies to perform its work. Consultants from Framework Partners in Planning, Inc., provided extensive orientation and process guidance, as well as specific types of technical expertise when needed. In this way, a team of faculty, staff, and students—guided by process and content experts—was able to effectively engage an entire campus in the consideration of major change.

Setting Context and Direction

The CTF focused on two types of activities: extensive scanning of our external environment and intensive dialogue with members of the university community. Scanning activities included development of a current profile of the university, assessment of macroeconomic forces impacting the institution, and assessment of the needs of key groups such as learners, researchers, and essential partners. The CTF conducted an assessment of key trends and issues related to essential resources (financial, technological, and human). They also conducted a comparative analysis of other advanced education providers, including other universities. Finally, they assessed the university's specific strengths, weaknesses, opportunities, and challenges. The results of these efforts were provided to the university in published form to assist in discussion of our strategic options.

The dialogue with the university community became a major feature of CTF work. Methods involved public forums and town hall meetings, workshops to deal with specific issues, small group meetings with campus leaders, presentations of key research findings, faculty focus group discussions on institutional strengths, daylong planning sessions with deans and other senior administrators, and a multiple-day retreat for academic department heads. Communication of findings was accomplished by first recording and returning the results of all discussions to participants, and then by publishing summaries of findings in the university newspaper. More than two thousand members of the campus community were directly consulted in the process, which lasted from midsummer to the end of 1996.

Developing the Institutional Strategic Direction

Using this extensive foundation of research and opinion, the CTF captured and refined a series of core institutional realizations and aspirations through additional meetings with campus groups. This work resulted in development of a two-page document entitled "Our Strategic Direction to the Future," which was presented for consideration by the academic legislative body (the general faculties council) and the board of governors in December 1996. The document was overwhelmingly approved by both groups and has now become the guide to lead the institution into further phases of redesign and change.

The Strategic Direction

Two important fundamental changes to our environment were recognized in this document. The first: "Postsecondary education is rapidly becoming a highly competitive and globally expressed enterprise. We must be a focused institution with a marketing strategy and a global presence. Traditional sources of financing cannot sustain our research university, but many new opportunities are available for providing financial stability. We must reconceptualize our financing in this new knowledge era."

Additionally, a particularly significant institutional strategy for accomplishing our goals was articulated: "Achieving and sustaining highest quality in our core activities requires the development of strategic partnerships and collaborations with other universities and educational providers throughout the world, with businesses and the professions, and with governments."

Finally, four principles to help guide the university in sharpening institutional focus were highlighted:

1. Affirm and strengthen institutional focus on our unique role as a research university.
2. Realign undergraduate curricula to serve learner needs for the knowledge era.
3. Focus and align graduate research programs to achieve and sustain international reputations for quality and innovation.
4. Postdegree continuous learning is a newly realized opportunity for the entire university, and a particular responsibility in light of the needs of the Calgary community.

Redesign and Change

In early January 1997, the university established a series of redesign and situation assessment teams, again drawn from faculty, staff, and students, to develop plans for implementing change in a number of high-priority areas. These areas were chosen to be of importance to the entire institution and to signal change to our internal and external communities. Chosen areas are curriculum redesign and teaching and learning delivery; recruitment, admission, and registration of undergraduate students; institutional positioning; information resources; revenue and expenditure strategies; research and graduate programs assessment; and library and scholarly communications assessment.

These teams will work in a coordinated manner and complete their design and assessment tasks in order for the university to plan for implementation of key changes before the end of 1997. Again, the process is being characterized by large-scale involvement with the university community. In this way faculty, staff, and students have full ownership of the process for setting and implementing our new strategic direction.

To further examine the University of Calgary's vision for the Knowledge Age, visit their campus via the Internet at their Web site (http://www.ucalgary.ca).

HOWARD YEAGER is associate vice president of academic planning at the University of Calgary.

GAYLA ROGERS is associate professor of social work at the University of Calgary.

DONNA FINLEY is external facilitator in the visioning process at the University of Calgary.

From a remote location in the Blue Ridge Mountains, Virginia Polytechnic Institute and State University, along with the Blacksburg Electronic Village, is setting a global standard for distributed learning through its Cyberschool Initiative.

The Cyberschool Initiative: Virginia Polytechnic Institute and State University

Earving Blythe

Virginia Tech is located in Blacksburg, Virginia, home of the Blacksburg Electronic Village (BEV). Despite its rural and remote location, Blacksburg enjoys the highest level of Internet usage of any town or city in the United States. This case illustrates how Virginia Tech's Cyberschool Initiative is leveraging the forces of transformation in this setting:

- The vision of the BEV and the Cyberschool Initiative create "vision pull."
- Campuswide training introduces Knowledge Age tools, on a rolling basis, for all faculty.
- A powerful information technology (IT) infrastructure is being developed, and pervasive training and resources for learning innovation using technology are being provided.
- IT infrastructure and faculty development processes are being redirected.
- A heavy investment is being made in virtual classes, "snippets of learning," and integration with BEV.
- A faculty culture is being created that is supportive of technology-rich learning.

This chapter provides a summary of the ongoing Instructional Development Initiative at Virginia Polytechnic Institute and State University (Virginia Tech). It describes the results of the workshops conducted for faculty, outlines the status of classroom upgrades, and presents examples of course restructuring.

NEW DIRECTIONS FOR INSTITUTIONAL RESEARCH, no. 94, Summer 1997 © Jossey-Bass Publishers

The Instructional Development Initiative began with three pilot faculty workshops during the summer of 1993 and continued with additional workshops through July 1995. Six hundred fifty faculty from seventy-six academic departments have now participated in thirty-eight customized workshops. The initiative is a large-scale effort to invest in our faculty by providing them with the opportunity to rethink their teaching and explore the potential of instructional technology for improving the effectiveness of the teaching and learning process.

With the support of the university president, Paul E. Torgersen, and Provost Peggy S. Meszaros, this initiative is intended to provide the opportunity for all faculty to participate, at some point in a four-year period, in an intensive workshop centered on the integration of instructional technology into the curriculum. In conjunction with the nine academic deans, the provost selects the mix of faculty attending the workshops each year.

Evaluation of the workshops by the faculty attendees continues to be positive. Faculty clearly value the opportunity to explore instructional issues with their colleagues and to discover the potential of technology for enhancing their teaching. They have indicated that these resources are critical if they are to adapt to the needs of their students.

Early results of surveys of students and faculty involved in classes that have been restructured as a result of this initiative show strong support for these new approaches to learning. Active learning is facilitated both in the classroom and outside, and constructive collaboration among students is encouraged. Technology promotes communication outside the classroom, primarily via e-mail. There is evidence that these efforts have had a positive impact on students' understanding of and interest in the course material; at the same time, the efforts promote better class attendance. In addition, students believe they are being provided more opportunities to develop skills that transcend the subject matter, including problem solving and critical thinking.

Faculty Development Institute

Faculty development workshops have been conducted for 650 participants as a continuation of a long-term strategy to provide faculty with the knowledge and resources to take advantage of the use of instructional technology in their teaching. The primary goal of the workshops is to provide an opportunity for faculty to reexamine curriculum issues and instructional methods that would allow them to adapt to the changing needs of students. These four-day workshops provided the time and resources for faculty to investigate alternative instructional strategies designed to improve the productivity of the teaching and learning process. As a result of attending the workshops, faculty participants receive a state-of-the-art computer with an Internet connection and a suite of appropriate software applications.

The provost, in conjunction with the college deans, selects the mix of faculty attending workshops each year. Faculty were grouped by curricular interests, with some workshop groups representing a single academic department and other groups representing up to eight disciplines. Steering committees representing participants in each workshop met individually with workshop facilitators over several months to custom-design their workshops.

Each workshop included training on a core skill set, comprising basic computer skills, electronic mail access, electronic resource access via the Internet, an introduction to multimedia, and design principles of computer-based instruction. To the extent possible, these core sessions were tailored to each group, with the customizing meant to involve faculty in accessing electronic resources of particular interest to them. For example, human resources participants learned how to access databases at the U.S. Department of Agriculture and the National Science Foundation, and to access national census and demographic data. In similar fashion, the introduction to multimedia was presented with examples of existing multimedia software that targeted general interests of each group. The veterinary medicine faculty were shown clips of software illustrating concepts in genetics, chemistry, and medical problem diagnosis.

Beyond the core skills, many groups focused on discipline-specific software. For example, the Department of Mathematics is currently engaged in large-scale experimentation with instructional modes that include technology in classroom presentations as well as interactive computer laboratory work. The aim is to overcome conceptual barriers and thereby broaden, by an order of magnitude, the range of students who succeed in making mathematics an effective tool for later course work and careers. At the same time, this new approach allows problems of a more realistic character to be brought into even elementary courses, speeding the transition to professional-level work.

Similar curricular discussions were conducted among other faculty participants. For example, faculty from multiple disciplines involved with design concepts (including architecture, art, apparel design, landscape architecture, and theater arts) examined and debated the use of computer-based tools to enrich two-dimensional and three-dimensional design instruction. Other groups chose to supplement their introductory sessions with more in-depth sessions on specific aspects of multimedia development and use. For example, communications studies and political science faculty were very interested in using, editing, and creating video segments. Most workshops included general sessions attended by all participants in the group and breakout sessions that permitted participants with different experience levels or interest areas to focus on topics appropriate to them individually. In addition to gaining a basic understanding of the computer-based tools themselves, faculty also spent time during the workshops discussing and debating with each other the possibilities for using technology to facilitate student learning.

The instructors for the workshops included information systems staff from educational technologies, computing center services, and the library electronic reference group, as well as faculty and staff from English, math, veterinary medicine, engineering, architecture, theater arts, art, music, and humanities. A variety of multimedia concepts and tools were introduced, including use of

CD-ROM databases, digitized video and audio resources, and multimedia publishing. Open lab time was provided to give faculty the opportunity to practice working with material from sessions and to begin working on new course materials for the 1995–96 academic year. These introductions set the stage for more extensive faculty training on specific tools that continues throughout the year.

Principles used in designing the 1995 workshops were developed from the feedback received during the 1994 sessions. The pilot workshops were conducted in May and June 1993 for three groups of faculty, from English, math, and humanities respectively. These initial departments were selected by the provost's office because they play a key role in teaching core curriculum courses with high enrollment and therefore have the greatest potential to affect large numbers of students in courses that are integral to the basic educational goals of Virginia Tech. In this phase, visiting scholars from other universities led discussions on redesign of courses using instructional technology. The scholars had performed early work in introducing Perseus (a humanities database of ancient Greek texts, images, and maps, as well as a survey textbook, encyclopedia, and Greek-English dictionaries) and Mathematica (software with numerical, graphing, and symbolic computation capabilities) into the curriculum at their respective universities. The English faculty received hands-on experience with an integrated writing tool, Daedalus, for developing undergraduate writing skills, as well as an introduction to Storyspace, a tool designed to enrich student learning through a hypertext environment.

These software tools were explored and used by faculty in the humanities, math, and English departments during the subsequent academic year. As a result, local expertise was developed and drawn on during the 1994 workshops. English faculty presented Daedalus sessions not only to their colleagues in English but also to human resources, social science, and humanities groups. Math faculty presented Mathematica to their math colleagues as well as to the physical science group. In this way, faculty could interact with their peers to understand the software capabilities and learn from the early implementation experiences. This also facilitated cross-curricular dialogue, as when the physics and geological science faculty discussed introductory calculus prerequisites for their courses with the math faculty who teach freshman calculus using Mathematica.

A real benefit, which goes beyond the specific departments involved in the workshops, is related to the mathematics department's support of students in the College of Engineering, which has already adopted Mathematica as a standard part of the students' software package. Engineering had requested that the math department introduce the software in calculus courses. The workshops conducted over the past two summers have provided an excellent opportunity for the math faculty to learn the software in a timely fashion and enabled them to scale up its use by students in more than fifty calculus sections during 1995 fall semester. The plan is to incorporate the use of Mathematica in all sections of the freshman-sophomore calculus sequence for students in science and engineering majors. In addition to promoting more effective teaching strategies, this prepares students to use the powerful software in more advanced work in engineering and other scientific disciplines.

Early Outcomes

One of the most significant outcomes during the early stages of this initiative has been the development of Cyberschool, which is a fusion of computer-interactive classroom methodologies, traditional classroom practice, advanced multimedia programs, and distance learning. It is conceptualized as a virtual campus, which breaks the mold of credit for contact and thereby meets the needs of a diverse student body over the next decade and beyond. It is a response to the need to teach more students without additional resources in terms of the number of faculty and classroom buildings. The Commonwealth of Virginia has projected an increase in higher education enrollment of seventy-five thousand students over the next five years while at the same time reducing resources allocated to higher education. As a response to these projected enrollment increases, Virginia Tech's plan for restructuring the university calls for application of instructional technology in the beginning to solve these problems.

Cyberschool will be implemented in three phases, with early courses being developed in the College of Arts and Sciences, the university's largest college. Resources have already been reallocated within the university to accomplish this goal. The Instructional Development Initiative, a four-year, $10 million investment in the faculty and classroom infrastructure, allows the university to leverage technology to accomplish its goals. The early phases concentrate on high enrollment and core courses.

The courses targeted for the first phase of Cyberschool include calculus, English, biology, and communications. Pilot courses were taught during the summer of 1995 in an on-campus environment. During phase two, the courses will be taught at educational centers around the state using appropriate technologies over a high-speed network linking these centers to the main campus. Phase three will provide the opportunity for wider dispersion of the courses statewide and beyond.

Early success has been achieved in two courses: communications research and civil rights. Faculty were given release time during the spring semester to develop Cyberschool courses for the summer of 1995. Instructional design specialists, programmers, and graphic artists provided support in restructuring the selected courses. The results of these pilot efforts showed in very positive student evaluations. These results are being used to assist in designing the second phase of the plan. Finally, phase three courses will be restructured for statewide implementation. The question to be answered is whether the use of instructional technology can provide alternative solutions while still maintaining quality and improving access without adding substantial cost.

Virginia Tech is already investing substantial resources in this project and plans to continue this investment. The initiative provides faculty development workshops, improved student access to computing, classroom upgrades, and support for course development activities. The university also recently received a grant from the Sloan Foundation to continue work on development of asynchronous courses, and to study the effect of this new paradigm on faculty productivity and quality of life. The cost effectiveness aspect of this work draws from the early efforts of Massy and Zemsky (1995).

The anticipated outcomes include improved student productivity in terms of student learning, greater access to core curriculum courses in the face of greater demand, and more cost-effective course delivery during a time of diminishing resources.

Future Plans

The Instructional Development Initiative is part of Virginia Tech's Phase Two plan for restructuring. The long-range plan for this initiative is to offer an opportunity to all faculty members on a four-year cycle. The goals outlined for the 1994–1998 time period are structured into three components:

I. Faculty development
   A. Provide the opportunity for all Virginia Tech faculty to participate in this faculty development program. The overarching goal is to motivate them to investigate, create, and utilize alternative instructional strategies.
   B. Provide participants who complete the program with access to state-of-the-art instructional technology, the knowledge to use it, and the motivation to collaborate with their colleagues in leveraging instructional technology in their courses.
II. Student access
   A. Provide advice to all students on their investment in computer technology in order to maximize its usefulness during their college career.
   B. Provide better access to computing resources for all students who do not have their own personal computers, and provide computer labs for accessing specialized software unique to disciplinary areas (such as Perseus, Mathematica, and Daedalus).
   C. Provide network-based training materials for students to ensure that they have a basic foundation in use of computing and instructional technology resources.
III. Course development
   A. Support faculty in developing network-accessible courseware and instruction.
   B. Facilitate development of electronic libraries of scholarly materials supporting designated courses.
   C. Provide improved classroom and presentation facilities to support faculty efforts in introducing new technologies into core curriculum courses.

Challenges and Opportunities

As faculty learn how to leverage the use of technology in instruction, they will be supported in redesigning these courses to provide new options for students, options that include electronic access to the faculty during nonclass hours as well as to course materials, references, tutorials, simulations, and on-line testing as appropriate.

Faculty are assuming new roles in designing, developing, and delivering instruction in a new educational environment. This use of technology provides options for students to more efficiently master the content of the course. As a welcome side effect, such use of information technology also provides students with much greater facility with advanced computer applications, experience that the corporate world increasingly views as one of the "basic skills" for college graduates.

Electronic access provides the opportunity for students in a variety of settings, lifestyles, and age groups to enroll in these courses. Putting students and faculty on the network simultaneously enables faculty to monitor students' progress during the course and provides immediate and much more productive feedback as their work progresses. Too often, students in large classes speak rarely or not at all, because of shyness or inability to articulate their questions as well as more verbal or aggressive classmates do. These barriers can be removed by opening up asynchronous modes of communication such as e-mail, electronic office hours, or computer conferencing.

This greatly enriched learning environment enables students to proceed at their own pace in problem-oriented subject matter, and it creates options for faculty to concentrate on problems being encountered by students in the class. Enhancement of the teaching and learning process ultimately enables faculty in more advanced courses to concentrate on improving students' higher-level cognitive skills.

These new teaching and learning options provide the opportunity and motivation for faculty to devote more time to designing course materials and to become more available to interact individually with students at a higher level of problem-solving activity. Under this scenario, students may become more independent learners as they interact with course materials, while at the same time benefiting from faculty expertise and experience in mastering course content and solving real-world problems. As a result, the students acquire learning styles and attitudes that are critical to becoming successful lifelong learners.

Students will eventually be able to interact with course materials without being encumbered by the traditional credit-for-contact model. Thus, the current practice of distance education is transformed as students both on and off campus take advantage of courses designed with the flexibility to meet diversified needs. Physical adjacency to classrooms, labs, and libraries becomes less important than electronic access to these resources. Particularly successful strategies have the potential for implementation at other universities.

Reference

Massy, W. F., and Zemsky, R. "Using Information Technology to Enhance Academic Productivity." *EDUCOM*, 1995.

EARVING BLYTHE is chief information officer of Virginia Polytechnic Institute and State University.

*The University of Minnesota, Crookston has transformed
its environment in a number of ways, including the introduction
of a notebook computer environment.*

A Notebook Computer for Everyone: The University of Minnesota, Crookston's Technology Strategy

Donald Sargent, Richard Heydinger, Tom Jorgens

The introduction of notebook computers provided the University of Minnesota, Crookston with a powerful instrument for leveraging change. It has meant introducing campuswide mobile computing, creating a vision of mobile computing as a means of campus differentiation, opening broad discussion of the initiative, creating a mobile computing culture that changes the way faculty and students interact and learn, and developing mobile computing products on the part of both faculty and students.

The University of Minnesota, Crookston (UMC) is one of the pioneers in making a universal commitment to using computing technology and information networking across its learning environment. In 1993, after more than a decade of gradually expanding the use of computing systems, UMC took the dramatic step of providing notebook computers to all of its full-time students and faculty. It also launched a major effort to create the networks that would link them to one another and to the world.

This decision was a key outcome of an intense strategic planning effort that featured a vision of expanding self-directed learning within UMC's polytechnic baccalaureate programs. The vision emphasized a future where the mobile power tools of the Information Age encourage and enable lifelong learning. Underlying the overall strategy was a clear message from employers that the ability to use the tools of the information society and to continue the learning process was a basic expectation for graduates beginning their careers.

The Notebook Computer Technology Environment

A key to making the technology strategy work was the choice of a mobile system, the IBM Thinkpad® notebook computer. The computer used during the period described in this chapter was the IBM 701 CS notebook, with color monitor, modem, sound, and Ethernet card. The notebooks were preloaded with Microsoft Windows 95 and Office 95 and Netscape Navigator. A technology access fee of $300 per quarter was added to the tuition and fee schedule for all students; it finances the computer equipment, software, and access to local information resources, including the library, the Internet, and free printing.

All faculty, staff, and students have e-mail addresses and are on the local area network (LAN). Fifteen classrooms were remodeled to include Ethernet and electrical connections at each student's seat, a digital overhead camera and projection unit in the teaching station to connect the faculty notebook into the server system, and a printer. Residential-life students have Ethernet connections in their rooms. The common areas on campus have similar connections. More classrooms continue to be remodeled to provide Internet access.

A help desk, staffed from early morning to late night, serves as the distribution and service center, provides warranty service, checks out notebook computers for part-time students, and is a place for everyone to go for problem assistance. The campus instructional technology center aids faculty in reviewing various software and equipment and providing some training programs. There is dial-in access to the campus network for faculty and students when they are off campus.

Reviewing the Progress

After three years of experience, signs of a dramatic change are widely observable. Students use their portables to take notes, communicate with faculty, prepare reports and presentations, access information, and solve problems. Reliance on notebooks is readily apparent in the student lounges and dorms, where students are often found working in teams. Most faculty members use their computing technology in a wide variety of ways to provide enhanced learning experiences for students. Nearly everyone on campus, from beginning students to senior administrators, uses a notebook and the network to communicate, share information, and automate routine tasks. As the campus day comes to a close, the mobile systems continue to be in demand; Internet peak use now occurs during the evening.

To measure the results of its technology strategy, UMC conducted a survey of both students and faculty during the winter quarter of the 1995–96 academic year. This survey provides baseline data to be used for future comparison. The student survey included returns from 177 students in the second-period class. Twenty-eight of the fifty full-time faculty responded. The survey results suggest fairly rapid progress in meeting the initial UMC goals of putting advanced learning tools and people together, developing the skills of lifelong learning, and moving the norm toward universal literacy in information age technology. It is equally apparent that the forward race of technology requires a deep commitment to continuous improvements in both technology and technology-related learning.

Assessing the Student Experience

UMC students were asked to respond to questions about benefits they gain from having the technology, the extent and diversity of their use of major applications, and their perceptions of overall impacts on their education and career preparation.

How Students Rate the Benefits of Notebooks and Networks. When asked to indicate the benefits of the new technology environment, the great majority of UMC students indicate that they receive major benefits. Almost nine out ten students reported multiple benefits. As shown in Figure 6.1, the strongest perceived benefits come from building technology skills that students associate favorably with career preparation. They also perceived gains in the quality and efficiency of their learning experiences. An example of this is evident from the 87 percent of students who indicated that they are able to do their work more quickly and achieve greater accuracy, with 75 percent reporting a perceived increase in the amount and quality of learning.

Figure 6.1. Major Benefits of Notebook Computers Reported by Students: 1995–96 UMC Student Survey

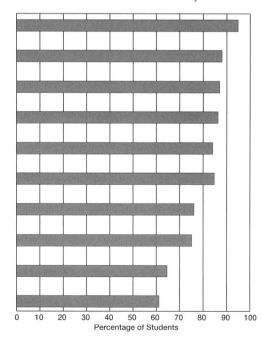

Build the technology skills I need in my career

Make progress toward goals as a UMC student

Complete my work accurately in less time

Improve research and information gathering

Use technology in creative problem solving

Take my work with me and do it when I choose

Work together with other students on projects

Increase the amount and quality of learning

Communicate with my instructors and get help

Manage class assignments better

0 10 20 30 40 50 60 70 80 90 100
Percentage of Students

How Students Use Notebook Computers and Networks. As shown in Figure 6.2, the use of computers and networking reflects the diversity of students and programs at UMC. The most popular applications reported by students are writing papers, completing assignments, sending e-mail, and entertainment. Note taking, information searches on the Internet, and self-directed learning and communicating with faculty and other students also ranked high in frequency of use. UMC students illustrate a growing level of sophistication, with approximately 50 percent of the students using spreadsheets, presentation graphics, and problem-solving applications.

How Students View the Impact of the Notebook Computer Technology Strategy. Students also validate several of the key assumptions behind the UMC technology strategy. For example, Figure 6.3 indicates that two out of three students said they believe their prospects for getting the job they want after graduation are enhanced by their UMC experience. Four out of five students indicate that they have gained in ability to continue learning after graduation, as a result of exposure to technology. Nearly one-half the students indicate that the technology commitment of UMC was a factor in their decision to enroll, and again almost one-half said that it influenced them to stay at the school to pursue a degree once they were enrolled.

Figure 6.2. Most Frequent Student Uses of Notebooks from 1995–96 UMC Student Survey

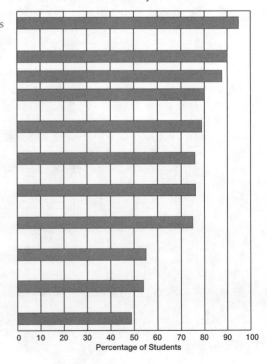

Write papers or complete out-of-class assignments

Entertain myself during my free time

Send and receive e-mail messages

Explore and develop my ideas and interests

Explore and use the Internet/World Wide Web

Find research materials and information

Take notes or complete other assignments during class

Ask questions of my instructors or fellow students

Work on solving math, science, business, or other problems

Complete or develop and use spreadsheets

Develop graphics and/or presentations

0   10   20   30   40   50   60   70   80   90   100
Percentage of Students

Figure 6.3. Percent of UMC Students Indicating that the Notebook Computer Improved Various Student Experiences: 1995–96 UMC Student Survey

The notebook computer has strengthened:

My ability to continue learning after I complete my degree

My prospects for getting the kind of job I want when I leave

My decision to stay at UMC and pursue one or more degrees

My decision to enroll as a student at UMC

My choice of a major field and future career directions

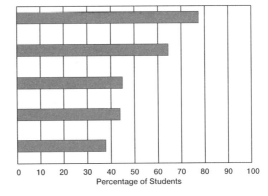

Percentage of Students

Several of the students who were interviewed personally confirmed these survey results. A UMC student from Winnipeg, Manitoba, said, "The biggest impact is that we are looked upon as the pioneer, and it is a source of pride. It was a big factor in my choice to come to UMC." An older student noted, "If you have a strong understanding of technology, you have a great advantage in business." She indicated that UMC's technology commitment was a big factor in her decision to return to school and in her decision to pursue a career in the information technology field. A freshman commented that, "A lot of students come to UMC because of the technology."

Assessing the Faculty Experience

Widespread use of computing technology by the college's faculty became common during the 1980s, and by 1987 all full-time faculty members had desktop computers. During this time, faculty members were encouraged to incorporate computing technology into their teaching, research, and outreach. Their experiences helped build support for larger commitment to integrating technology into the educational process. In 1994, all faculty were provided with notebook computers. In the 1995–96 survey, faculty were asked to assess both campus and personal experiences since the time when the notebook technology commitment was implemented.

How Faculty View the Impact of the Notebook Computer Technology Strategy. There is agreement among the UMC faculty on the impact of the notebook technology. As shown in Figure 6.4, 90 percent of faculty report that student opportunities for project learning have increased. The large majority of UMC faculty perceive significant changes in the way they teach and are actively involved in developing new materials and tools that take advantage of the technology.

**Figure 6.4. Percent of Faculty Responses Noting a
Major Impact of Notebook Computers on the Learning Environment:
1995–96 UMC Faculty Survey**

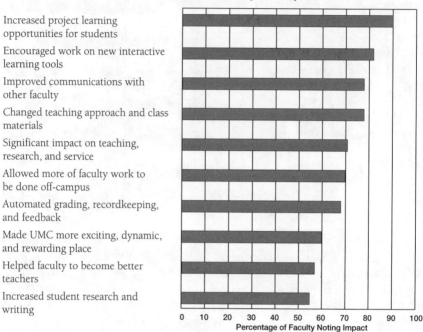

Improvements in intrafaculty communications and off-campus work were noted. Sixty percent of the faculty indicated that UMC has become a more exciting, dynamic, and rewarding place to work as a result of the technology commitment.

How Faculty Perceived Changes Linked to the Notebook Technology Strategy. The most pervasive changes on the campus as reported by faculty are directly linked to use of technology. Technology skills and computer literacy have expanded across the campus. Faculty members feel pushed to keep ahead of the skills and expectations of students. The majority report increased communications with students and other faculty, as well as linkages with other colleagues (Figure 6.5).

There is considerable evidence to suggest that the most significant short-term impact is in reallocation of time to different kinds of activities. For example, both this survey and personal observations corroborate an increase in communication between students and faculty. At this stage, the majority of the faculty do not perceive an increase in productivity accruing from the technology. That is not surprising, given the fact that faculty have been making the requisite and considerable personal investment of time and energy in skill building and innovation.

Figure 6.5. Faculty Reported Changes Resulting from Notebook Technology Strategy: UMC Faculty Survey 1995–96

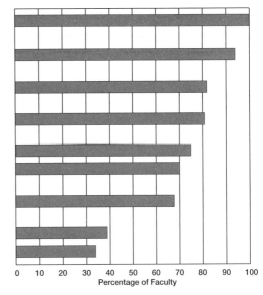

Expanded the computer technology skills of the faculty

Pushed faculty to learn technology to stay ahead of students

Expanded teaching and learning opportunities

Strengthened the image of UMC for faculty

Fostered linkages with other colleges

Increased the ability to stay current on field

Increased communicatings among faculty and students

Boosted faculty productivity

Increased collaborative teaching

0 10 20 30 40 50 60 70 80 90 100

Percentage of Faculty

How Faculty Used Computing Applications. Routine use of computers and networks for word processing and electronic communications has become universal at UMC, with nearly everyone doing so daily. Probably this could be said about many campuses today. However, at UMC 90 percent of the faculty are now reporting regular use of presentation software; spreadsheets; and topical, field-related software. Nearly all faculty also report using the resources of the Internet and electronic libraries, technologies that were not readily available three years ago (Figure 6.6).

Although there is widespread use of the general tools, usage among faculty falls off for more specialized tools, as Figure 6.7 shows. There is anecdotal evidence that these rates are also accelerating.

Conclusions

The 1993 commitment that the University of Minnesota, Crookston made to providing all students and faculty with notebook computers has had an immediate and dramatic impact on the teaching and learning environment. Most importantly, students find renewed self-confidence as they approach their careers, prepared with up-to-date technology skills and an approach for life-long learning. Faculty have made the time investment required to expand their own skills and reexamine their teaching.

These major conclusions can be drawn from the UMC experience:

**Figure 6.6. Regular Computer Uses Reported by Faculty:
UMC Faculty Survey 1995–96**

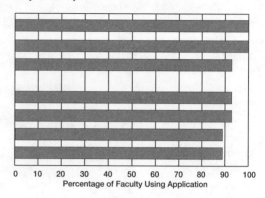

Word processing (e.g., Word)

e-mail (Pegasus Mail)

Other topical softward related to your field

Presentations (e.g., Powerpoint)

Spreadsheets (e.g., Excel)

Internet/World Wide Web

Library searches

Percentage of Faculty Using Application

- Putting notebook computers in the hands of students and faculty, coupled with widespread access to networks and standardized core applications, has proved to be a broadly effective educational strategy.
- Students place high value on the skills and experience with technology that they gain at UMC, and they plan to carry that forward into their careers. As a result, student use of technology is at a high level.
- Faculty members have generally moved quickly to adopt new technology and incorporate it into the teaching and learning environment. Growing innovation has become evident.
- It is important to identify early faculty innovators. They need support and are the key in adoption and implementation of the technology strategy.
- Support systems that make technology user-friendly are critical to success at UMC. Simple high-benefit applications are adopted quickly by both students and faculty, followed by more complex, specialized uses.
- The "anytime, anywhere" features of portable computers necessitate dial-up networks with a comprehensive technology support system, and multimedia capable classrooms with Ethernet and electrical connections to students' seats.
- Students are gaining valuable self-directed learning skills as a result of having twenty-four-hour access, easy-to-use systems, and encouragement to work together with other students.
- The essential financing of computer technology can be successfully accomplished using technology fees when the value-added benefits to the student learning experience are understood by the faculty and students, as in a full partnership.
- Adopting a successful technology strategy requires commitment to reallocation of funds with each unit budget to implement the notebook network technology strategy; it also means an ongoing commitment to keep technology current and to continue building technology capacity, along with critical training and support.

Figure 6.7. Common Computer Applications Reported by Faculty: UMC Faculty Survey 1995–96

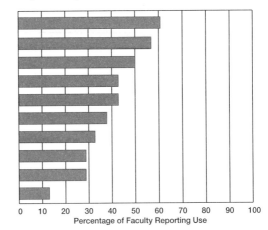

The mobile computing model figures prominently in the university's plans for the future.

Looking Ahead

The original goal in implementing the notebook technology at UMC was to strengthen the teaching and learning environment so that students became self-directed learners with the ability to use the tools of the information society. Even though great strides have been made toward that goal, there are some remaining challenges:

- There must be an increasing investment in instructional development to utilize constantly changing technologies and accommodate different learning styles.
- Upon high school graduation, large numbers of students have not developed the discipline necessary to master learning outside the classroom setting.
- Technology investments must continue to be balanced with productivity or other value-added outcomes.
- New educational services for the information-based society utilizing mobile notebook technology need to be implemented as part of the institution's programs and services.
- More students are entering college with computers and with greater differences in levels of technological skill. Thus institutional technology strategies need to be modified every year.

Technology initiatives require continuous attention. They just may be the catalyst needed by higher education institutions to retain their role in the education provider industry.

DONALD SARGENT is chancellor of the University of Minnesota, Crookston.

RICHARD HEYDINGER is partner with the Public Strategies Group, Inc.

TOM JORGENS is president of MetaDynamics, Inc.

Arizona Learning Systems is a cooperative effort of multiple community colleges, creating a new learning enterprise that will provide virtual learning resources to be integrated into the offerings of participating community colleges. The intent is to create a virtual branch campus of every community college district.

A State-Level Catalyst for Transformation: Arizona Learning Systems

Doreen Dailey, Thomas Hassler

The Arizona Learning Systems (ALS) initiative is transformative in every way. It enhances change initiatives in the community of Arizona Community Colleges:

- A vision for virtual, competency-based learning to complement physical learning
- Broad discussion across all campuses regarding the development of ALS
- Development of an information technology (IT) interactivity infrastructure and commitment to its use
- Redirection of campus planning processes to reflect ALS
- Development of competency-based distributed learning material
- Creation of a new learning culture to support ALS

Arizona Learning Systems is an alliance of Arizona's urban and rural community colleges, whose purpose is to provide learner-centered education environments that build on the unique advantages technology affords the learning process. A task force designing ALS is currently addressing two major goals: (1) expansion and upgrade of telecommunications lines to connect learning sites throughout the state of Arizona through a contract with a private (common) carrier, and (2) reform of higher education practices to meet the emerging needs of all Arizona residents for perpetual learning, as well as development, application, and evaluation of new and powerful learning strategies.

ALS is engaged in designing a framework whereby:

• Arizona community colleges will be able to import and export courses, certificates, and degrees across current district boundaries, thus allowing students access to a significantly greater array of learning options than what is currently available in any given district. This includes access by high school students to higher education learning options, allowing them to fast-track acquisition of skills and knowledge.
• Arizona community colleges will be able to export programs out of state, thereby allowing them to act as entrepreneurs and generate revenues to supplement state and local funds in meeting increased demands of in-state learners.
• Arizona community colleges will partner with K–12 schools, Arizona's universities, private business, and related government agencies to consolidate the number of high-speed telephone circuits among sites, resulting in dramatically reduced costs to support a statewide telecommunications infrastructure. Agreements for sharing information technology resources will be forged, regulatory barriers removed, and operating costs shared.
• Arizona community colleges will contribute to statewide economic development through expansion of "information highway" services and facilities to allow Arizona residents to compete in the digital economy of knowledge workers.
• The competitive edge of Arizona businesses will be increased through access to learning-on-demand, to assist employers in remaining on the cutting edge.
• The name *Arizona* will become recognized in the international educational and economic markets.
• Arizona Learning Systems will act as an "attractor" to pull transformation in higher education through unique course standards and student support practices and by modeling the transformation of work practices for the Knowledge Age.

ALS has received funding and support from the Arizona legislature (as discussed in the section "Why Was Arizona Learning Systems Formed?") and is moving forward, as this chapter seeks to illustrate.

There are three main characteristics that differentiate ALS from most other virtual learning initiatives. First, *the existing institutions are important.* ALS depends on existing community college districts to give its offerings a connection to local communities and existing learning enterprises. It creates a perpetual, distributed learning environment that combines virtual and physical learning resources.

Second, *innovative cultures are built within existing organizations.* The existing community colleges are the base for ALS. There is no need for a new, totally independent learning enterprise if existing institutions can create parts of themselves that can change rapidly enough to retain the public's confidence that they can meet society's educational needs.

Third, *funding is based on usage.* After initial start-up, the funding to individual ALS units will be based on their success in generating utilization. This will create a market for ALS products and services.

Why Arizona Learning Systems Was Formed

Conversations among Arizona community college presidents indicated interest in sharing resources to stretch dollars in support of direct service to students and to provide mutual support for change in their respective organizations. In August 1995, the Arizona community college CEOs endorsed drafting of a legislative request to connect individual district telecommunication systems to one another to support statewide delivery of learning opportunities.

As a result of this request, the state's FY 1997 Appropriations Act contained a provision that appropriated $1.1 million to the State Board of Directors for Community Colleges as a special line item. Of this sum, $100,000 was a one-time grant to (1) design a statewide plan for interconnecting and consolidating community college, university, and K–12 telecommunications, video systems, and voice and data systems, and (2) tie individual community college districts' electronic delivery systems together. The additional $1 million was provided to begin implementation.

Support for this initiative was enhanced by development of the Western Governors' University (WGU), a consortium initiated by the governors of several western states to address projected dramatic increases in the need for higher education access throughout the region. In addition, the governors have expressed concern that higher education serve the needs of working adults and employers. The WGU's May 1996 implementation plan reported that the two primary functions of this virtual university were to "broaden access to higher education by fostering the use of advanced technology for the delivery of educational services and to provide formal recognition or certification of learning achieved, regardless of sources."

Additional funding for ALS has been moving forward. In February 1997, an additional $7.5 million was requested—months after the regular budget process was completed. Much of this request was justified on the basis of establishing technology-assisted learning. These initiatives demonstrate the powerful sense among Arizona legislators and legislative staff of the need for decisive action to meet the learning needs of the twenty-first century. The ultimate form, structure, and funding of ALS are still to emerge.

The Arizona Context

The state of Arizona is representative of many western states in that it has a large geographic area but a relatively small population mostly clustered in two major metropolitan centers and the remainder in small communities across the state.

Higher education needs are addressed by three state universities, ten community college districts, and a small number of private institutions of higher education.

Arizona's ten community college districts (with eighteen separately accredited community colleges and more than fifty additional outreach learning centers) have had to pioneer a variety of strategies to meet the learning needs of placebound working adults as well as citizens residing in small communities with large geographic barriers and distances from urban and rural education sites. All of the community college districts have had to address these issues. To take four notable examples:

Arizona Western and Mohave Community Colleges have linked their distance delivery systems together and jointly offer a "weekend college" electronically.

Rio Salado Community College, in the urban Maricopa District, has significant distance-delivered course options as well as an associate's degree program that is to be delivered on the Internet as of early 1997.

Northland Pioneer Community College, whose service district includes the Navajo, Hopi, and Apache reservations, offers the associate of arts degree via interactive video classes at eight campuses and centers.

Yavapai College has been delivering coursework using interactive television for nine years and has an extensive array of telecourse offerings and new Internet courses in the graphic arts. The college has also developed multimedia materials to support classroom instruction as well as asynchronous learning options, and it has an exemplary learning assessment program.

In addition to these examples, *Northern Arizona University* has pioneered the development of technology infrastructure and innovative instructional techniques to deliver upper-division and graduate courses throughout the state via interactive television.

Thus, from the start of ALS, there have been examples around the state of significant pioneering efforts in distance delivery and technology assisted learning. But they have operated in isolation as "islands of excellence" with no systemwide acknowledgment or support. Furthermore, many of these examples—although significantly far from Carnegie unit, placebound offerings—have still suffered from being but one step ahead of merely digitizing historical instructional methodologies.

In summary, a variety of factors converged to set the stage for a bold initiative to transform higher education in Arizona: recognition by policy makers of the need for higher-quality, cost-effective, new paradigms to meet the perceived future demand for learning; a culture of innovation among community colleges throughout the state; rapid emergence of the western states' consortium to develop new models for cooperation and delivery of higher education through a virtual university; and support from the state board for community colleges and the community college CEOs to explore new options.

Arizona Learning Systems Design

The design of ALS coalesced around several core ideas, some of which are extensions of other schools' efforts, and some which are new and unique, as we now highlight.

Organization and Governance. ALS will function as a "virtual" branch campus of every community college district in the state and be governed by a board consisting of a representative from each community college district. This virtual campus will have limited staff and draw on faculty from each institution as well as using RFPs to supply the learning options or courses. Tuition and state reimbursement will be split between the institution originating the course and the *home* institution with which the student is affiliated.

Student Institutional Affiliation. Students will enroll in courses taught through ALS by way of the community college associated with their geographic location. This ensures using just one transcript, regardless of the origin of the course and allows a long-term advising and mentoring relationship to be established with the individual learner. This further establishes the framework for perpetual learning and builds on the inherent connections of community colleges within their communities.

Asynchronous Learning Options. Learners will be given a variety of options for achieving competence, including desktop learning options at home or through local learning centers that remove restrictions of time and place.

Course Standards. ALS course standards assume that content will meet the rigor and general requirements set forth by regional accrediting bodies and promote transformation of instructional practices through some additional elements. Courses should be student-centered, flexible in design, and built on the advantage of local resources; they should use the community as a laboratory and build critical thinking and the ability to learn and work collaboratively.

Integration of Pedagogy and Technology. Development of technology infrastructures has frequently preceded readiness to change approaches to teaching and learning. ALS focused first on desired learner impacts, second on how they can be supported with new applications of technology, and last on the hardware, software, and standards.

Critical Process Elements in Emerging Planning and System Design

Designing a new concept and its operating processes requires strategies that are symbolically resonant with the desired system. We now identify some of the key planning elements in the ALS process.

Task Force and Participant Selection. Rather than appointing task force members on the basis of geographic or constituent group representation, members were solicited from among the community college CEOs according to their ability to think creatively and represent the entire system. A fortunate by-product of this selection technique was a team that works exceptionally well together and shares leadership responsibilities.

ALS sought people who could work with large amounts of rapidly changing data and integrate it. The ALS committee process includes expanding committees that draw additional members from around the state when input is required in specific topical areas; the committees then shrink to the eight-member team to integrate the information and apply it to the design of the system.

Building on Existing Culture to Ensure Credibility and Ownership. It was decided that the design team would be the primary builder of the new system rather than delegating that responsibility to consultants. In this way, the group brought the history and organizational cultures of Arizona's community colleges to the process from the beginning. Using the tenets of *participatory design*, the design team's tacit knowledge and domain expertise became powerful drivers of a model that is innovative and yet politically and culturally acceptable.

Facilitation of Evolution in the Group Process. Because ALS needed to effect rapid, early success in a realm having no pathfinders, nontraditional group facilitation techniques were employed. Within a framework of project-deliverables, group facilitation allowed a significant amount of self-organizing; for example, members would volunteer for committee membership and assignments, dyads and triads of team members would spontaneously form to pursue the in-depth development of a concept, leadership at all levels would shift as circumstances required. In this way, a face-to-face collaboration resembling "network scholarship" unfolded. For the design of new systems, it is essential not to let group members come to closure too quickly, lest they act on old assumptions. Rather, an appropriate balance must be kept between "mental meandering" and producing a product.

Structure of the Work. This was completed in intensive bursts. Meetings lasting two or more days were scheduled that gave structured time for individual reflection and writing, with individual products brought back to the larger group for consideration. Electronic communication was maintained in the weeks between these meetings. The interludes between meetings allowed gestation time for ideas but were not so long that ideas and focus diffused.

Furthermore, from funding to implementation, the first ALS-delivered courses were created in seven months. This fast track was critical in ensuring rapid, highly visible success as a catalyst for further development. To be certain that this goal was achieved, it was determined that ALS would select a narrow path utilizing only the highest-quality, distance-deliverable courses as a harbinger of future offerings.

Consultants. Consultants were used by ALS in two ways: to design specific components for ALS, and as catalysts for the group's thinking. To maximize planning grant resources and augment project credibility, ALS sent their plan to expert readers around the country for critical review, thereby avoiding parochial thinking. Stipends of $500 were paid to state community college faculty members and staff to develop position and operation papers. This yielded quality products while increasing awareness of ALS and internal community college cohesion.

Consultation Groups. To ensure broad-based input, members of the ALS design team met with standing groups around the state, including chief academic officers, information technology directors, county superintendents, and representatives from a variety of state agencies.

Communications Structure. Integral to the ALS project structure was a communications plan that included a monthly newsletter, an e-mail listserv, a World Wide Web page, and teleconferences, as well as strategic face-to-face meetings with key policy makers.

A Model for the Transformation Process

There are a number of common hurdles in implementing a change program in higher education:

- Comfort with the tried and true
- Political and economic costs of risk taking, particularly in the public sector
- Lost productivity related to resistance or low morale when change is perceived as being thrust upon a group
- Reluctance to adopt anything "not invented here"
- Fear of long-term commitment before a strategy has proven useful
- Difficulty moving from values to a system architecture that supports those values

Most importantly, for transformative change to occur there must be a mechanism for "out of the box" thinking, because professionals are methodically aculturated to draw on what they know in problem solving. However, invention of new systems is not a problem to be solved by looking back. The following are change model strategies that address common barriers.

Challenging Assumptions. *Transformation* implies more radical change than do the incremental or continuous improvement strategies that have made their way into higher education in the past few years. To effect transformation, it is essential to have a willingness and ability to challenge deeply held assumptions. As Peter Senge, of the Massachusetts Institute of Technology, stated in a workshop, "We don't know what fish talk about, but we're certain it isn't water." That is, what we are culturally immersed in is invisible to observation unless we can achieve a different vantage point through deep inquiry. As the ALS task force tackled the issue of learning assumptions, at times the group used the total quality management technique of asking "Why?" multiple times. One notable example was the assumption, familiar to community colleges, that small class size is essential to a quality learning experience.

As the group struggled through the *why,* what eventually emerged was the importance of student-student and student-teacher interaction, not class size per se. Discussions about the role faculty expertise will play in this new environment indicated that faculty are one of many sources of expertise, and that what learners need is to have tools for information analysis. Through this process, a new set of learning assumptions emerged that could then be used as the theoretical basis for new methodologies and approaches.

Transition Strategies and Emergent Planning. As the need to fuse work and learning intensifies and technological options change at an accelerating pace, it is imperative not to be deluded into thinking we are designing a model of higher education for the next one hundred years (as the development of land-grant colleges indeed served our country for the past one hundred years.) Rather, technological change and learning needs require ongoing redefinition of what constitutes best practices in learning. Therefore, planning must be seen as an emergent process rather than one in which goals are framed in an inflexible, deliberate strategy. In the traditional higher education culture, there is a tendency to perceive plans as long term and constant change as reflecting indecisiveness on the part of leadership. It is critical to communicate reforms in higher education as transition strategies—rather than as ultimate solutions, which risks resistance when additional change is called for within two or three years.

Transition strategies include moving from the traditional classroom's unidirectional conveyance of information to the highly interactive, self-directed learning strategies of the transitional period. The latter moves toward Donald Norris's concepts (1996) of mass customization and perpetual learning built around long-term mentoring relationships with faculty.

Achieving Critical Mass. One of the dilemmas of change processes is whether to attempt to move everyone in an organization to the new model or whether to select the innovators and isolate them in a supported environment. ALS serves as a catalyst for the reform of higher education by achieving a critical mass of innovators that cuts across individual institutions. For example, if each community college district had only ten innovators, able and eager to offer learning in the new model, this group would constitute about one hundred faculty statewide. By connecting these otherwise isolated groups of innovators, a critical mass can be formed with significant potential impact. This exemplifies the power of technology to create *communities of interest* and accelerate development and implementation of innovations in learning. Thus ALS itself becomes a model for network scholarship. Furthermore, because entire faculties in existing institutions are not being impelled to change, the likelihood of major resistance coalescing is diminished. As research suggests that most faculty are very pragmatic in nature, change is more likely to be accelerated in the broader organization as a result of proven success on the part of the innovations. In the terms of quantum physics, ALS will serve as a "strange attractor" that pulls movement toward improved practices rather than pushing against the inertia of comfortable positions.

The Paradox of Ownership and Control. A classical dilemma of transition strategies is whether change can be initiated from within or whether one must go outside the organization to achieve the desired ends. ALS has adopted a paradoxical model in which change is effected both inside and outside the community colleges. The description of its governance defines ALS as a virtual branch campus of every Arizona community college district, a university within a college. Thus each existing community college district plays a role in governing ALS. Simultaneously, the virtual community concept creates an *innovation college,* operating outside the boundaries of the existing campuses. The ALS innovation college will have its own course standards, which are more demanding than those of most community colleges; its own programming criteria based on market demand; and unique personnel policies governing its contributors.

Within this paradoxical structure, the advantages of initiating change within a new structure are gained along with those of transforming existing entities of higher education.

Visit the Arizona Learning Systems home page at their Web site (http://www.als.cc.az.us). There you will find a description of ALS, a library of their publications and information, the complete development plan of ALS, and white papers on the various programs developed by ALS.

Reference

Norris, D. M. "Perpetual Learning as a Revolutionary Creation." *On the Horizon,* Nov.–Dec. 1996, pp. 1–4.

DOREEN DAILEY *is president of Yavapai College.*

THOMAS HASSLER *is dean of information services at Northland Pioneer College.*

The development of the University of Delaware's student services building has been the most visible outcome of an eight-year program of improving administrative services provided to its students. The university has integrated cutting-edge technologies into the whole fabric of student life, instruction, communication, and administrative support.

Technology, New Facilities, and Organizational Realignment: The University of Delaware

David E. Hollowell

The University of Delaware used its investment in technology to enable and catalyze a fundamental change in its approach to student services:

- Investment in information technology (IT) infrastructure—specifically, networking and administrative software—enabled fundamental changes in facilities, processes, and organizations.
- Several campus processes were redirected to transformative ends: facility planning, restructuring, and infrastructure development.
- A vision of one-stop shopping for student services was established, eventually to be "no-stop" shopping for many students.
- The campus culture was fundamentally changed to focus on one-stop shopping, cross-functional services, and increases in the professionalization of campus student service workers.

These changes were not introduced as part of a bottom-up transformation initiative. In a sense, they were "stealthed" into the campus, a choice of term appropriate to the early 1990s when the initiatives were launched.

Institutional Context

The University of Delaware is a privately chartered, state-assisted research university, consisting of ten colleges offering 114 undergraduate-level, 72 master's-level, and 38 doctoral-level degree programs. The university enrolls about twenty-one thousand students, primarily from states along the Boston-Washington corridor. Approximately seven thousand of these students reside in university housing.

As recently as the late 1980s, the university enjoyed the luxury of having more applicants than it felt were needed. It was able to attract a freshman class in increasing numbers and of reasonable quality, employing a modest admissions program and minimal financial assistance. Computer support for admissions, billing, financial aid, housing, and registration were modest to nonexistent. Even more disturbing than the lack of computer support were the bureaucracy that students faced to accomplish even the simplest administrative tasks and an institutional attitude that improving services to students was not a priority.

A student attitude survey administered in 1987 identified several areas that ranked below average compared to others in the survey and compared to national norms. These areas included general registration procedures, financial aid procedures, billing and fee payment procedures, dining services, attitude of nonteaching staff toward students, and concern for students as individuals. These deficiencies made clear the need to address not only systemic issues but also attitudes of employees.

Substantial Leadership Change

The time period from 1988 to 1990 was one of substantial leadership change at the university. An administration in place for nineteen years had presided over the doubling of enrollment and significant growth in academic and research programs, but the administrative support for student, business, and other services had not kept pace. The challenge for the new leadership was not just to consolidate and build upon the academic advancements but also to improve the service and efficiency of support systems and to develop the tools needed to better manage the institution in the years ahead.

I was recruited to the University of Delaware in January 1988 with a mandate to improve administrative services in every area and to develop management systems that would better support ongoing operations, management, and institutional planning. Given the survey results and the critical importance of enrollment management, the first priority was clearly student-related information and services. The focus of this paper is on the transformation of student services at the University of Delaware and the role technology played in that process.

To go back to the late 1980s, the student service units on the campus were, with few exceptions, very inward-focused. There was little teamwork and cooperation among the departments, nor was there a perceived need or incentive for such cooperation. Students were bounced from office to office and stood in long lines to accomplish the semesterly ritual of enrolling at the university. Some of the student service units had a reputation as being uncaring, even downright unpleasant, in dealing with students.

It did not take an in-depth management review to determine that a major change in approach was imperative. Although the overall plan would take longer to develop, it was clear that inability to provide better service and much of the perceived and real staff attitude problems were due to the lack of tools to get the job done. Simply put, people often did not have the information needed to do their jobs in a timely and efficient manner.

Changing the Information Systems Infrastructure

In April 1988, a student information system steering committee was appointed, chaired by the registrar and with senior representation from the offices of admissions, billing and collection, financial assistance, housing, institutional research, and management information systems. The basic charge to this committee was to guide conversion and development of student-related administrative systems. The immediate goals were to develop functional specifications for an integrated student information system; evaluate software packages available in the marketplace; compare such products to an in-house MIS development plan; and recommend an action plan within six months.

Initially, the dynamics of this committee were interesting to watch. Some members shared the view that an integrated system was unnecessary. The committee spent its first few meetings figuring out how to work with one another and then to developing an understanding of each other's issues and problems. As time went on, the concept of a team approach matured as members of the committee came to understand that many of their problems were held in common, or caused by discontinuity of procedures from one office to the next.

In September 1988, one month ahead of schedule, the committee made its recommendation that a student information system produced by Information Associates be acquired and installed. A project schedule and a funding plan were developed, and the recommendation was approved by the president in October 1988, with a two-year implementation goal. The contract was signed with Information Associates in December 1988, database conversion began in August 1990, and the system went live in October of that year.

In this start to the process, several key goals were established: (1) emphasize quality and efficiency of service, (2) develop a team approach among both management and staff, and (3) develop the tools needed to get the job done. As the process evolved, several objectives emerged under each of these goals.

One objective was to apply technology to its fullest advantage. By 1988, the university had already made significant investments in computing technology and begun to install a campuswide fiber optic network. Any system to be developed would have to be fully online and capable of being accessed by departmental offices and, where appropriate, students themselves. The university also made investments in a database environment that would permit integration of what were five separate and redundant systems into a single, comprehensive database system with which the user could easily navigate from one area to another.

Teamwork

As mentioned earlier, the success of this endeavor is dependent upon the cooperation of several units and teamwork at both managerial and staff levels. The steering committee, and eventually various project teams, focused on overall goals and objectives, subordinating those of individual units. A major objective was not to accept past practice without question. The results were changes to many archaic policies and streamlining of many procedures in order to achieve efficiencies and make the processes more user-friendly.

With the units involved reporting to four different vice presidential areas, it was essential to have a sponsor, at the level of senior vice president, with clear support from the president. The steering committee knew that it had direct access to those who were able to change policies and procedures or even reorganize functions if that were necessary to get the job done. It is important to note, however, that this project did not begin with an assumption that the organizational structure of the university needed to change. Rather, the focus was on process and how each student service procedure could be simplified, streamlined, and made more student-friendly.

New Leadership and a Newly Operational Information System

The year 1990 was significant because a new president was appointed and the student information system became operational. Implementation of the student information system during the 1990–91 academic year proved to be very successful. Staff in the offices were trained and quickly became comfortable with using the system. Even before it was installed, concepts for how it could be distributed more broadly were being devised. Clearly, the new system could be used to foster change as it provided tools to support new and innovative services.

Even in the student information system's first year of operation (1990–91), selected college and departmental offices were tied into the system to support a variety of applications: advising, course scheduling, drop and add, and senior check-out. By fall 1992, all colleges and departments had access. Many of the faculty are now using the system directly to access class lists, student schedules, and transcripts.

Training

Another major activity that supports this effort has been training. From the start, the issue of helping university staff better serve their clients received attention. Programs in improving interpersonal skills and telephone manner were provided. As the systems became available in test mode, staff began to receive training on their use. As an integrated, menu-driven system, the student information system is very easy to use and has the power and flexibility for one person to answer questions that may involve information from two or more areas. For example, a person answering a billing question can look at a student's registration record to see the specific courses listed, examine details of a financial aid award, and determine the basis for room and board charges through simple navigation from one screen to another.

Redirecting the Student Information Systems Committee

Having the tools gave the university a basis on which to develop better and more efficient means of supporting students and those people who interact with students regularly. The student information system steering committee was not discharged once the system went live; rather, it has continued to monitor the effectiveness of the system and identify additional ways to improve the effectiveness and efficiency of student services.

An Opportunity to Relocate and Realign

One of the issues identified by the committee had to do with the physical location of the various student service offices. They tended to be scattered and not well arranged to provide efficient service even with the tools then available. In the summer of 1991, a small, centrally located building of about 11,400 square feet became available; it was judged appropriate to serve as a centralized student service facility. One advantage of this building was that it was a single-story shop building that needed total renovation if it were to be used for any other purpose. So the plan was to gut the building and lay out the interior from scratch.

Selecting Functions for Realignment

The challenge was to select the functions that would be best served by relocation to this building (since it was not large enough to house student service offices in their entirety) and to design a layout that would provide efficient service. The registrar was once again asked to assemble the steering committee to consider the issue. The initial reaction of the committee was to bring in the architect to begin laying out the space, but this notion was rejected. The committee's instructions were to take a step back from current thinking and focus on the objective that students who visit the facility should be served as efficiently as possible. This mandate included the novel notion that the student might be able to satisfy his or her question without talking to a single person. If that was not possible, then the student should be served by only one individual whenever practical. Again, the committee was reminded of the goal of using technology to its fullest advantage.

The committee began to analyze the kinds of questions and processes that caused students to visit their offices. They also considered what parts of their activities were essentially back-office functions that could be separated from those directly serving the public. The committee determined that about 20 percent of the people who visited their offices did so to accomplish very simple activities such as picking up a registration or financial aid form, getting a copy of their class schedule, learning the status of a loan application or student account, or requesting an unofficial transcript. About 60 percent of the questions were routine and could be answered by a person trained to access information in the various components of the student information system. Only about 20 percent of the questions required the assistance of a specialist in a particular student service area.

List of Items and Services

Given this information, the committee developed a list of items and services that should be provided in the lobby area of the new building. Some were as simple as having racks with clear signs indicating where students could pick up various forms and information booklets. Others were easily available using the technology that led to development of "kiosks," where students sign onto the system using their student ID and a personal identification number and access their class schedule, academic record, financial aid record, and billing information on a read-only basis. By adding a printer, students can print their class schedule or an unofficial transcript and be on their way.

For routine activities, the idea was to have a service counter staffed by personnel who were cross-trained in various student service areas (generalists). In those cases where a specialist was needed, that person should be located within sight, and in close proximity to the generalists.

As these concepts evolved, issues were overcome, such as an initial belief that individuals could not possibly be cross-trained well enough to serve as generalists or that more staff would have to be hired. There were already individuals who essentially served full-time on the front counter, and the system provided the tools needed for one person to answer a wide variety of questions. Proper training would be the key.

Developing a Floor Plan

With this groundwork accomplished, the architect was then brought in to lay out a floor plan that would meet service requirements. There was some skepticism among the managers and staff involved. To help turn that skepticism to enthusiasm, the president called a meeting of all the staff who would eventually occupy the building. The meeting began in a classroom, where the president offered his views on the importance of serving the students well; it then proceeded to the student services building, which at that point was a gutted shell. Set up inside the space were drawings of the layout, exterior elevations, and furnishing and fabric samples such that the concepts and physical realities could begin to merge in people's minds. In the months that followed, visiting the building to monitor construction progress became a favorite lunchtime walking destination for many of the people who are now housed there.

The building floor plan is shown in Figure 8.1. For control and audit reasons, the cashiering function is separated from the other service functions, but the staff in all areas received the same training such that a cashier is often able to answer questions about the source and nature of a charge without having to refer the student to another individual. The training program involved having staff rotate through the various offices so they could see firsthand the work of each office and the kinds of information that they process. In addition to the small number of individuals whose primary duty is to staff the front desk, students are often used to serve as generalists; other individuals in each area were identified and trained to provide backup during peak times.

The building houses the entire billing, collection, and cashier function; student telephone services; portions of the registrar, dining service, and financial assistance operations; and, at peak times, staff from the parking and housing offices assist at the counters.

The student services building opened in August 1992. It has been received extremely well by the students who have used it. Already the university has found ways of adding other services in the building without requiring more staff.

Since 1992, efforts have continued to expand access to the student information system to all those on campus who are involved in the advising process and to make available, across the campus computer network, the kinds of information initially obtainable only on the kiosks in the student services building. Data are currently being loaded into the system that will permit advisers and students to access progress toward degree requirements or to determine what additional courses may be needed if a student wants to change majors. Several colleges at the university are already using this function with good success. Installation of a voice processing system in 1993 has permitted students to register, drop and add courses, renew library books, and even get grades by simply using a touch-tone telephone.

An Eight-Year Program of Service Enhancement

The ability of academic departments and advisers to access student information to answer questions and improve advising is having an impact, as has installation of the interactive voice response system using the touch-tone telephone.

What the University of Delaware has accomplished both in the area of student services and in its applications of technology has not gone unnoticed beyond the campus. Since the student services building opened, more than forty colleges and universities have sent well over one hundred people to see the building and hear from our staff about what we have done. In 1995, the University of Delaware received the CAUSE Award for Excellence in Campus Networking. This award not only recognized the university's ubiquitous network but focused on how the technology is an integral part of campus life,

Figure 8.1. University of Delaware Student Services Building

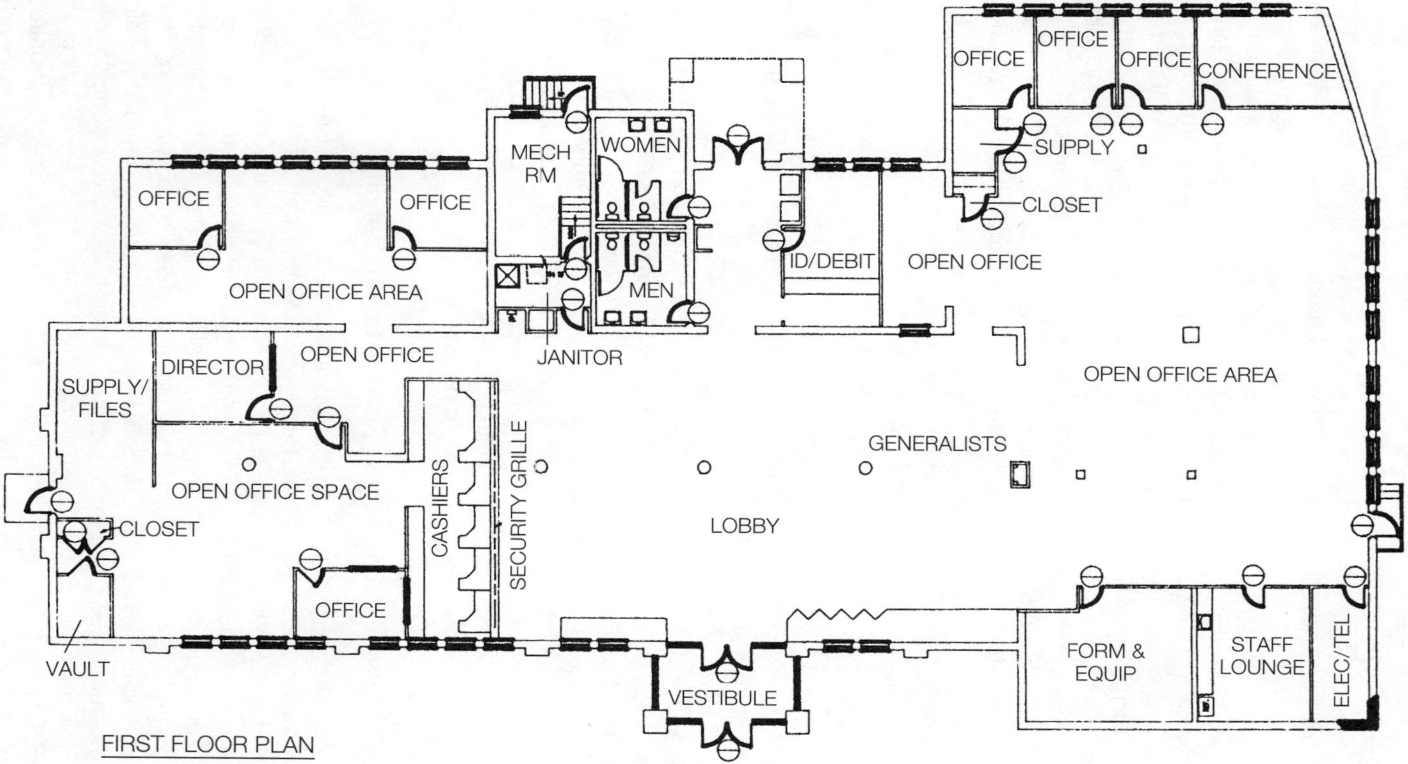

FIRST FLOOR PLAN

enriching the experience of every student. The university has integrated cutting-edge technologies into the whole fabric of student life, from the perspective of support for instruction, communication, and administration. Technology has clearly facilitated transformation in many aspects of the university's operations.

Future Directions

Where do we go from here? We continue to distribute access to the system more broadly on the campus and will eventually permit greater student access to the system as network and system security issues are resolved. The World Wide Web offers new opportunities for applications development that can further improve delivery of services to the university community. As examples, hundreds of students and potential students have taken advantage of Web-based forms to apply for admission or apply for campus housing. We have already seen the role of the generalists reduced by half, as the Web and other online services have replaced the need for students to seek assistance from the staff.

This paper has focused on development of the student information systems and student services building, but these activities are only part of a larger focus on the lives of our students both in and out of the classroom. As budgets are reduced, the most significant cuts have been in those administrative areas having the least impact on instructional units. A major facilities renewal program has focused on classrooms, residence halls, dining halls, and student recreational facilities, including a sports and convocation center that opened in 1993 and a new student center that opens this year (1997). Services such as campus dining, bookstore, residence hall laundry operations, and personal computer maintenance have been outsourced, resulting in better service with financial advantages accrued to the institution.

Benefiting the University

How has all this benefited the students and the university? Based on last year's satisfaction survey and general observation, students are responding well to our efforts. Although there are very few students still at the university who recall how these services performed in 1988, there have been enough changes annually that the juniors and seniors can easily see the improvements. Time will tell if their increased good feelings about the university will translate into alumni support. We believe that our efforts to be technological leaders and a student-centered campus are responsible for a multiyear trend of increasing applications, including significant growth in our honors program. The faculty, staff, and administration at the university can now take pride in being able to provide responsive levels of service thanks to the investments made in systems, facilities, and training, and the hard work of many dedicated employees.

Visit the University of Delaware's home page at their Web site (http://www.udel.edu). There you will discover links to the university's colleges and departments, libraries, research centers, continuing and distance education programs, and campus life. Follow the Student Services link to receive a tour of the university's innovative student services building, including photographs of the new facility and a breakdown of all the services and activities it offers.

DAVID E. HOLLOWELL is executive vice president of the University of Delaware.

Northwest Missouri State University uses the Baldrige framework as a powerful tool for assessing organizational performance and developing a comprehensive strategy for improving it. The feedback recommendations from the Baldrige process spawned a number of initiatives having positive outcomes.

Building the Regional University of the Future: Northwest Missouri State University

Joseph E. Gilmour, Dean L. Hubbard

Northwest Missouri State University used a maturing continuous quality improvement (CQI) process as a centerpiece for its campus change processes. In this way, it leveraged the following forces of transformation:

- Use the campus CQI initiative to redirect all campus processes to a CQI-driven transformative focus
- Conduct campuswide dialogue on change using CQI as a focusing element
- Create a vision for a regional state university of the future
- Develop a quality-driven, learning-centered culture
- Develop mobile computing, faculty development, and new learning initiatives

The university is continuing to use the Baldrige framework to organize transformative efforts.

Becoming the Regional Institution of the Future

Northwest Missouri State University is a state-assisted, four-year regional university, offering bachelor's, master's, and specialist degrees in three colleges. It was founded as a normal school in 1905 and over the years has grown to university status. Today it serves sixty-two hundred students on its Maryville Campus and at off-campus locations throughout northwestern Missouri. Northwest has successfully adapted to a declining population base in its service area by drawing a greater proportion of its traditional students from Greater Kansas City, Southwest Iowa, and Southeast Nebraska, and expanding its outreach program in an historic nineteen-county service area. It has undertaken several initiatives that have successfully enhanced the economic development of northwest Missouri.

In recent years, strategic planning at Northwest has been driven by several imperatives for change, now widely recognized as relevant to all higher education: pressure for greater educational value at lower cost; greater responsiveness to educational needs, transcending the barriers of time and location; emergence of perpetual learning; the challenge and opportunity of information technology; and the need to demonstrate measurable results.

The story of Northwest, a hardworking institution seeking to become the regional university of the future, is very much a work in progress. The transformation initiatives described in this chapter stem from a tradition, which can be traced to the university's founding, of deep concern for the students it serves and success in their personal and professional lives. Building on this strong foundation, the university created a "culture of quality" in 1984 to foster and accelerate continuous improvement on the campus. From 1984 to 1991, this effort was aimed at identifying best practices on and off campus and deploying them in appropriate units of the institution. In 1991, realizing that this approach had reached its zenith, the university adopted the Baldrige Education Pilot Criteria[1] to continue the progress of the Culture of Quality.

The Baldrige Framework

The Malcolm Baldrige National Quality Award Program is a federal government approach to spur improvement of business and industry. The program, begun in 1987 and overseen by the National Institute for Standards and Technology, is best known for the Baldrige Award. It is given to business, industrial, and service organizations for extraordinary performance in terms of the criteria established as part of the program.

A pilot program is now under way to extend the award program into the health care and education sectors. Northwest participated in this pilot program and was privileged to be the only university to receive a site visit in the first round of the process. It also participated in the Missouri Quality Award Program, a state-level Baldrige clone, and received a site visit as part of the program in 1994–95. The current plan is to focus, in 1996, on addressing the feedback from the various visits and decide as a community whether to pursue the awards in future years. Because the North Central Association has agreed to allow the university to use the Baldrige application as the core of its 1997–98 self-study, it is likely that this application will be submitted to the Missouri award program in 1997.

The education assessment criteria developed for the program have been broadly used in slightly different form throughout U.S. business and industry to drive continuous quality improvement and reengineering efforts in organizations. Extraordinarily demanding, they are built on eleven core values and concepts that characterize world-class educational organizations:

1. Learning-centered education: placing the focus of education on learning processes and the real needs of learners
2. Leadership: recognizing the crucial role senior administrators play in the development of a student-focused, learning-oriented climate
3. Continuous improvement and organizational learning: becoming learner-centered requires well-executed continuous improvement processes that are embedded in the way an institution operates
4. Faculty and staff participation and development: understanding that the institution's performance depends on the capabilities and motivation of its faculty and staff through ongoing development and training
5. Partnership development: organizational success requires internal and external partnerships that are long-term and involve mutual investments
6. Design quality and prevention: placing much greater emphasis on effective design of programs focused on preventing individual failure and improving instructional processes and based on learning objectives aimed at meeting the individual learning needs of students
7. Management by fact: recognizing that a continuously improving organization can only know if its tactics and strategies are effective if it has sound measures of their impact
8. Long-range view of the future: the organization must anticipate the changing needs of its students and stakeholders, creating strategies for anticipating them
9. Public responsibility and citizenship: the institution must serve as a role model for its students and stakeholders with regard to public health, safety, and the environment
10. Fast response: increasingly, institutions will have to respond more quickly and flexibly to the needs of students and stakeholders, and reduce learning process cycle time along various dimensions including time to completion and assessment feedback to the learner
11. Results orientation: the institution should have a performance measurement system focusing on results that reflect and balance the needs of students and stakeholders.

This dynamic performance system is shown in Figure 9.1. Leadership serves as a driver for four interactive subsystems: information and analysis, strategic and operational planning, human resource development and management, and educational and business process management. These subsystems, linking with leadership, exert influence on school performance results and student focus and student stakeholder satisfaction.

The whole process is aimed at achieving three goals: student success and satisfaction, stakeholder satisfaction, and student retention. Northwest has set three universitywide "stretch" goals in line with them: (1) all students who

Figure 9.1. Education Pilot Criteria Framework: Dynamic Relationship

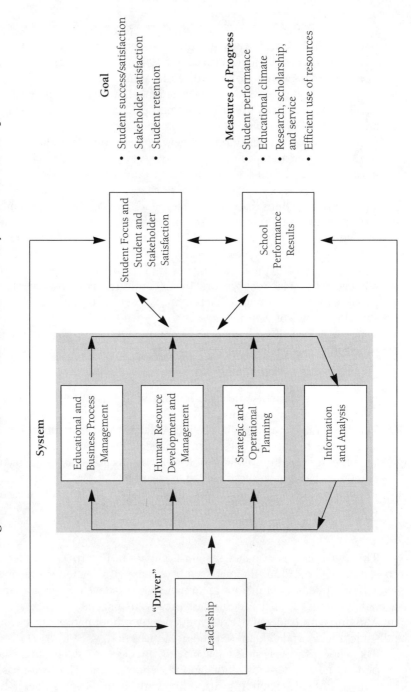

leave Northwest will have evidence that they have been uniquely advantaged by attending Northwest; (2) graduation standards will require that all graduates reach a minimum criterion-referenced level that ranks them in the top half of their national cohort group; and (3) in the context of increasing graduation standards, cycle time for learning and delivery of services will be reduced by 25 percent by the year 2000.

In this paper, we focus on efforts to develop and deploy approaches that address the critical feedback Northwest has received from its Baldrige and Missouri Quality Award site-visit teams. These include systematic, participative strategic planning; a seven-step process for operational planning of processes; a strengthened process for academic governance; a strategy for professional development of faculty; and creation of an information- and analysis-based approach for decision making.

Although none of these approaches is directly dependent on the others, we believe that implementation of the whole will result in performance gains that are much greater than the sum of the parts. Thus we are attempting as much as we can to move on the set in unison.

Strategic Planning

Strategic planning is at the core of Northwest's efforts to enhance its strategic position and improve itself. The Baldrige and Missouri Quality Award site-visit teams applauded Northwest's strategic planning process but noted that operational planning needed to be better aligned with it and that communications about organization directions needed to be improved. Figure 9.2 shows a newly designed university process for strategic and operational planning and implementation that is designed to address these criticisms.

The figure defines the role of key constituencies in the strategic planning process. As the bottom bar indicates, faculty, staff, and students are involved through all phases. The left-hand triangular figure at the top shows that the board of regents, assisted by a broadly representative strategic planning council chaired by the president and including seventeen members, has responsibility for university strategic planning. The council is assisted in its work by an extensive network of internal and external advisory bodies defined as "other voices." These are consulted by the council during its annual planning retreat and throughout the year on issues of pertinence to them. Careful and systematic consultation with those "voices" will be essential to obtaining a broad consensus across the university on basic organizational directions and for communicating the directions.

As the boxes underneath the board of regents/strategic planning council indicate, their roles focus on strategic issues. They examine the strategic context of the university in light of its mission and values, review organizational progress, and assess the status of its core competencies. From this review, they define the university's strategic options, update its vision for the future in mea-

Figure 9.2. Northwest Missouri State University Strategic Quality Planning Process

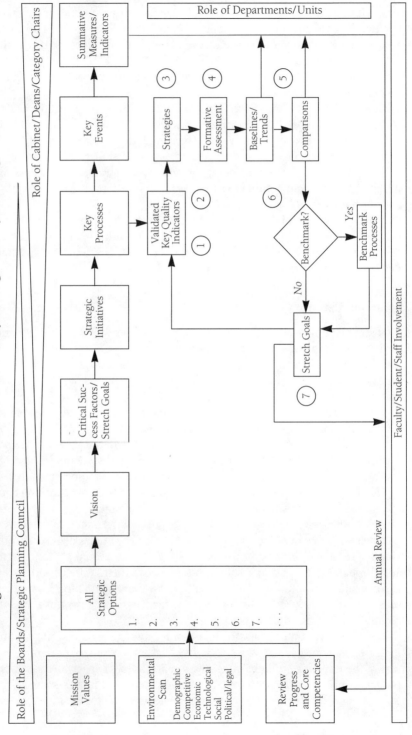

surable terms (stretch goals), and define and prioritize strategic initiatives to reach those goals. Much of this work is done at an annual three-day retreat in May attended by the planning council and representatives of the other voices.

The university's newest strategic initiatives include a major thrust to upgrade computing capability, entitled Electronic Campus Plus, open the Governor's Academy for Computing, Science, and Mathematics for high school students; and create a postsecondary educational consortium for Northwest Missouri with the University of Missouri and other regional institutions (including area vocational and technical schools) in which the Northwest will serve as the managing partner. Each of these initiatives moves the university toward the goal of extending its reach in the educational pipeline, becoming a key supplier of higher educational services in the future, and being sure that it has the wherewithal to take full advantage of information technology to deliver educational services.

As the right-hand triangle at the top of Figure 9.2 indicates, the president's cabinet, the deans, major department directors, and chairs of each of the seven Baldrige Categories take responsibility for implementing these initiatives. This includes defining the key processes necessary to accomplish the initiatives as well as the key events essential to making the processes happen, and using project management techniques to measure the extent to which key event timelines have been met. The results of this work are fed back into the planning work of the strategic planning council. Nested in and guiding this implementation process is the seven-step operational planning process, which is described in the next section.

Seven-Step Operational Planning Process

Northwest's seven-step planning process is designed to help all units plan and improve the processes for which they are responsible so that they meet the needs of their key stakeholders and are in alignment with the overall directions of the university. This process was identified by the Baldrige and Missouri Quality Award site-visit teams as a significant strength. At the same time, the teams called for its deployment across the university to produce sustained results and systematic tracking of stakeholder satisfaction. These are the seven steps in the process:

1. Identify key quality indicators
2. Validate them with the stakeholders
3. Develop goals and define deployment strategies
4. Formulate an assessment strategy to track performance
5. Establish baseline data, track trends, and do competitive comparisons
6. Benchmark superior processes (when appropriate)
7. Set stretch goals

Steps One and Two. A Key Quality Indicator (KQI) is an essential attribute of a program that indicates quality as perceived by the customer. (For example, Northwest's ten educational KQIs include such competencies as teamwork and team leading, communications, computing, problem solving, and academic major.) These steps involve identifying stakeholders; asking them what attributes they seek from the process being planned for; combining these attributes into an integrated list in the voice of the stakeholder, which is aligned with the university's mission and strategic directions; and validating and refining the list in a second conversation with stakeholders. For most processes, six to eight KQIs are identified.

Step Three. This step involves several tasks for each KQI. The first is to define one or more goals, which are interpretations of what the stakeholder requires in measurable terms. For each goal, one or more critical success factors (key and measurable objectives that must be addressed to ensure alignment with the university's strategic directions) are delineated. For all critical success factors a deployment strategy is developed, which identifies where the critical success factor will be achieved (for example, in courses or internship) and who is responsible for its achievement. The result for a given process (for example, an academic major) should be a coherent process that the stakeholders, the faculty, and the administration can clearly grasp, one they can see contributes to achievement of the university's mission. This is an area historically given short shrift by higher education and one that should be considered more both in terms of program coherence and reduction of student time to graduation through better design and understanding of program aims.

Efforts in this step can involve process reengineering. Indeed, Northwest's faculty senate has identified six learning precepts that its curriculum committee will study, building on work already done by Northwest faculty, to see if the precepts can be fit into an integrated learning model that yields significant advances in student learning. The precepts are active learning, assessment as learning, the faculty member as facilitator or mediator, norm-and criterion-referenced assessment, effective use of information technology, and application of CQI tools to the learning process. Our benchmark for this work is Alverno College in Milwaukee, Wisconsin.

Step Four. In this step, an assessment strategy is developed for each KQI, including both formative and summative evaluation. At least one measure is defined for each critical success factor. The key here is to develop measures (as few as possible) that are valid; this is a tall order and it often precludes use of standardized tests. The results of this assessment are fed into the university's strategic and operational planning processes to determine where continuous improvement efforts should be focused.

Step Five. This step involves taking the measures defined in step four and establishing a baseline, tracking progress of those measures over time, and developing comparisons with competitors. The idea is to improve on the baseline and in due course exceed the performance of competitors.

Step Six. This step involves efforts to significantly enhance process performance through intensive examination of a high-performing process either at a competitor institution or at an organization in another sector that has processes relevant to the one at hand.

Step Seven. A stretch goal is a target that cannot be reached by using the processes currently in place. Successful achievement of stretch goals generally involves benchmarking and reengineering.

Northwest is currently implementing the seven-step process in all units, which we see as the key to addressing many of the comments regarding process in the feedback from our Baldrige and Missouri Quality Award site-visit teams. The process is extraordinarily demanding in terms of intellectual effort and time, but it results in much clearer definition of processes; establishes a solid connection among these processes, stakeholder needs, and university mission and strategic directions; and places the processes into a continuous-improvement regimen.

Academic Governance

The Baldrige and Missouri Quality Award site-visit teams noted Northwest's need to capitalize more on the capabilities of empowered work teams and less on traditional, top-down distribution of academic governance responsibilities. The quality theory behind the recommendation is that quality-oriented organizational improvements can be "driven" into an organization to a point, but beyond that the values and tools of quality must be understood, embraced, and practiced at all organizational levels if the organization is to achieve the full potentials of continuous quality improvement. In response to the site-visit team recommendations, a report from a special committee that included five past or present faculty senate presidents recommended that academic departments be conceived as empowered work teams and that distribution of academic governance responsibilities be decentralized. In a nutshell, the new design is predicated on the concept that the principal role of administrators is to create and nourish an environment that allows the relationship between the student and faculty member to flourish—all in the name of enhancing student learning and lifetime success. The resulting structure gives faculty even greater control over circumstances in their departments (selection of team members and learning resources, nomination and evaluation of chair, etc.) while more tightly linking the departments to the needs of their students and stakeholder and university goals through the seven-step process.

Implementation of the new governance approach has been slow and tough going because it directly confronts the prevailing academic culture and challenges the traditional role and prerogatives of the academic administrator. A customized program has been created to assist administrators at all levels in developing an empowered work culture, drawing on established team development principles. (A parallel process has also been prepared for academic and administrative support units and is being adopted by them.) A decision has been made to move slowly on implementation of the new academic governance approach, starting with the dean's council and moving deliberately through the college chair councils to departments desirous of developing a team culture. We continue to believe that over time the essential elements of the approach will be adopted broadly because they contribute so much to high-level performance improvement.

Faculty Professional Development

Another key area identified as needing improvement by the Baldrige and Missouri Quality Award site-visit teams was alignment of faculty assessment and reward structures with the university's commitment to undergraduate learning and empowered departmental teams. Four departments from the three colleges have volunteered to develop and pilot a faculty development process that is in keeping with these requirements. The result will be a transformation of the traditional processes for faculty development toward one focused on making the faculty member successful; the new process assumes that the vast majority of those working in a department want to make a positive contribution to its success. The new approach will involve team goal setting in terms of the department's KQIs and evaluation in terms of the faculty member's role in the achievement of those goals by team colleagues. (The assumption is that the department KQIs are established with input from the dean and the vice president for academic affairs.) The new approach also allows greater flexibility for the department to capitalize on the individual strengths of the faculty member.

The four pilot departments will continue working on the new framework in fall semester 1996 and begin piloting it in fall semester 1997. They are very enthusiastic about the work they have done so far and are taking the steps they need to gain acceptance across the campus for the new professional development approach. The current objective is to determine the pilot's viability after two annual cycles. If these criteria are successfully implemented, they will move Northwest's academic culture significantly toward the empowered team culture envisioned in the academic governance approach and enable major strides in implementing quality principles across the university's academic structure.

Information and Analysis for Decision Making

The final key area identified for improvement by the site-visit teams was the need for university leaders to more systematically monitor and use information in providing leadership and to track and use information more systematically for improvement.

To address this criticism of the academic units, we have undertaken the development of an annual academic departmental assessment process. The process will have three major report components: (1) statement of department mission and vision, (2) seven-step process status report, and (3) analysis of department workload measures (using a five-year history and projection). The intent is for these reports to be concise, well organized, and developed in such a way that they can be used to track and compare departmental performance along a time dimension and with each other. Although these reports are designed in accord with Baldrige requirements, they will supplant a number of separate reports: departmental annual reports, the state coordinating board's five-year program review, and numerous ad hoc resource allocation reports. In addition, when the seven-step process is completed and juxtaposed with a consistent set of workload data in a series of reports available to all, the criteria by which resources are allocated will be clear and more likely to be perceived as fair and equitable.

Conclusion

The Baldrige framework provides a powerful tool for assessing organizational performance and developing a comprehensive strategy for improving it. At Northwest, we can already see the positive impact of our initiatives to address the Baldrige feedback recommendations in terms of enhanced commitment to the university's strategic directions and improved process design. By the end of the 1996–97 academic year, we anticipate having baseline measures for most processes. In succeeding years, we will be able to assess the extent to which our CQI approaches are enhancing performance and begin in earnest to set stretch goals in key areas. In today's challenging environment, we should do no less for our students and our stakeholders.

Visit the campus of Northwest Missouri State on the Internet at their Web site (http://www.nwmissouri.edu). There you will find general information about Northwest Missouri State's academic colleges, admissions, library and computing services, campus events, and outreach programs.

Note

1. National Institute of Standards and Technology. *The Malcolm Baldrige National Quality Award 1995 Education Pilot Program.* Gaithersburg, Md.: Author, 1995.

JOSEPH E. GILMOUR is vice president for academic affairs at Northwest Missouri State University.

DEAN L. HUBBARD is president of Northwest Missouri State University.

By dramatically redirecting its existing advising processes, Eastern Michigan University created an intrusive, technology-supported advising system that fused academic, developmental, and career advising. This approach is the centerpiece of the Career Horizons program.

An Intrusive, Comprehensive Advising and Career Planning System: Eastern Michigan University

J. Michael Erwin

In 1995, Eastern Michigan University developed an "intrusive advising" approach designed to improve student retention and student success by focusing on the process of helping students choose and prepare for careers. This approach leveraged the forces of transformation by redirecting existing advising processes; creating a new IT-based, fused advising system; being driven by a vision of student success based on fusion of learning; and developing a new learner-centered culture.

The advising approach is the core component of the Career Horizons program, a broadly focused array of interventions offered through the Division of University Marketing and Student Affairs and coordinated by the Career Services Center. The core component of Career Horizons is an advising approach that uses a "self-informing" student information system called the Personal Career Attainment Plan to monitor students' progress toward their educational and career goals. In so doing, the system succeeds in providing a focus for the advising efforts of the career center, the academic advising center, and faculty advisers.

Impetus for Creating the Career Horizons Program

Eastern Michigan University is a comprehensive, public university enrolling approximately twenty-three thousand students, more than eighteen thousand of whom are undergraduates. Like many public universities, Eastern's enrollment peaked in the early 1990s (exceeding twenty-five thousand students in

1992) and then fell roughly in proportion to the declining number of high school graduates. Impetus for the creation of the Career Horizons program can be traced, in large part, to Eastern's response to those declines and to its president's commitment to transform the university to a learner-centered institution.

The Linkage Between Retention and Advising

Spurred by dropping enrollment rates at Eastern, the university's board of regents made retention a principal institutional initiative, approving a strategic plan that called for creation of a universitywide retention council. In early 1995, the council issued a final report that included six major recommendations, two of which addressed the need to remove barriers to learning in the areas of student support services and student advising. In part, the recommendations called for systems to monitor student academic success that would provide continuous feedback to students on their progress, and for development and implementation of a plan for removing barriers to learning associated with academic, departmental, and career advising for students.

The President's Transformation Initiative

While the retention council was in the final stages of arriving at its recommendations, administrative efforts to improve student retention had been channeled in such a way as to revitalize the president's transformation initiative. That initiative began in 1990 when EMU's newly appointed president outlined his vision for transforming Eastern from a "teaching university" to a "learning university" by the school's sesquicentennial year 1999. Largely because of faculty resistance to what they viewed as the learning university paradigm's inherent diminution of teaching, by 1993 the strategic planning process was at a virtual standstill. However, in 1994 the president refocused his change effort from the learning university toward identifying and removing barriers to student learning, announcing his "barriers to learning initiative" in early 1995. An advisory committee was established and charged with monitoring progress toward one primary goal: "to enhance our students' ability to access educational opportunities, become involved in their educational experience, and attain their educational goals."

One of the first orders of business on the barriers-to-learning agenda was addressing the retention council's call for improved student advising. In spring 1995, two of the three sources of student advising, the academic advising center and the career services center, were asked to volunteer for reviews. The third source, faculty advisers in academic departments, were not asked to participate. The advising center and career center were each asked to use a self-study process to evaluate the accessibility of their services to students and then report to the barriers committee on the measures they proposed as means of increasing accessibility.

A New Approach

As staff of the career center finalized their self-study, the vice president of university marketing and student affairs began regular meetings with the career center to formulate a new, broader role for the center. The vice president had long had been convinced that a key to improving student persistence and learning is recognizing that students who lack career goals are less likely to succeed academically than students who have goals and plans for achieving them. What the vice president sought from the career center was a model that would place that office prominently in a divisionwide change effort aimed at helping students identify, clarify, and then achieve their educational and career goals.

Given the vice president's mandate for a new approach and the expectation of the barriers committee that it would play a vital role in student advising, the career center was positioned for campus leadership, if it could develop an approach that would overcome two significant constraints. The first and most obvious constraint was the number of students to be served. Increasing the amount of advising available to all of the more than eighteen thousand undergraduates would necessitate major realignments in staffing and programs of the career center and of any other units providing services. With additional funding and staffing unlikely, what seemed to be a quick though partial answer to the problem was a computer-based advising system.

A second major constraint was that, like many if not most other universities, Eastern's approach to student advising is fragmented among various advising centers and faculty advisers. No procedures or mechanisms existed for academic advising staff, faculty, and career center staff to share information about a given student. Since attempting to restructure the institution's fragmented advising process was viewed as impracticable, what seemed to be needed was a way of focusing the efforts of each party on the needs of a student as that individual progressed from one adviser to another. A portfolio approach for more than eighteen thousand undergraduates seemed unmanageable, but a computer-based student record was feasible.

Development of the Career Horizons Program

Although a computer-based advising system that would track the progress of students toward their goals was deemed necessary, a model or conceptual framework was needed to structure and focus the system. The most obvious framework to use would be a career development model. Career development models typically recognize three or four stages of progress, from lack of awareness and concern about a career choice to preparation for job entry. Most of the models also recognize student development as having educational, career, social, and personal dimensions. Typically, the models identify the decisions students need to make at each stage and in each dimension of development, and they then prescribe the experiences and skills students need to acquire.

Eastern's career center staff developed a career development model tailored both to the needs of EMU students and to the resources available at the institution. The model provided the framework for the Career Horizons program, a sequenced array of opportunities for students to identify and pursue their career goals. Like the models that shaped it, the program was envisioned as prescribing student use of resources available throughout the university and surrounding communities. Unlike the other approaches, Career Horizons would be *intrusive,* from admission to graduation.

Beginning with their attendance at Eastern's preorientation program for admitted students, students would be encouraged to think of their educational goals in terms of career preparation. At the preorientation and some months before matriculation, career inventories would be administered to determine each student's developmental stage. Information obtained from the student would be recorded in his or her "personal career attainment plan," or PCAP, a file in a relational database program that would match the student's developmental status with prescriptions for the specific actions the student should take.

The resulting prescriptions would be made available to students in two ways. For the first year or two of its use, PCAP prescriptions would be generated each term and mailed to students, initially by campus or U.S. mail and eventually, once all students had computer accounts, by e-mail. Prescriptions would also be available in a second, less intrusive format: a record students could view and update by accessing it on their computers. The screen version of the PCAP would include the decisions each student needs to make and the skills and experiences the student needs to acquire; it would allow the student to generate his or her own prescriptions for presentation as Web pages detailing a range of alternatives for acquiring the needed information, skills, or experience.

As they explored ways in which a prescriptive system like the personal career attainment plan could be used, it became apparent to Eastern staff that they could extend their tentative model in at least four ways. PCAP could:

1. Refer students with academic difficulties to tutoring
2. Incorporate the skills and experience necessary for each career field based on faculty experience
3. Include prescriptions to help students gain admission to graduate programs
4. Reduce costly marketing efforts through an easy-to-update computer-based system

Broadening the Array of Criteria and Interventions

Given institutional concerns that focused especially on the retention of freshmen and sophomores and the amount of time that would be required to work with faculty to develop their criteria for employment success, career center staff chose to pilot the PCAP with fall term 1995 FTIACs. In addition to piloting the PCAP, career center staff worked to broaden the array of criteria and interventions offered for 1996–97. Development focused on two areas: obtaining PCAP criteria and prescriptions from faculty, and Web site development.

Faculty Development of Criteria and Prescriptions

An underlying assumption guiding the design of the Career Horizons program is that if the PCAP is to fuse and focus the advising process, it must be embraced, shaped, and used by faculty. Accordingly, a high priority for the 1995–96 academic year was to begin the process of working with academic departments and programs to identify PCAP criteria and data elements needed to prepare prescriptions that assess student progress relative to the standards and needs of employers and professional and graduate schools. In addition to attempting to develop criteria and prescriptions, a critical need was to begin tightening PCAP's ability to match majors and careers by obtaining from faculty lists of careers that they viewed as related to their majors.

As a part of the earlier barriers-to-learning review, the career center had proposed and then committed to begin working with academic departments in 1995–96 to jointly develop plans for tailoring career center services to the needs of individual departments.

Although it would require extending completion of the PCAP into a third year, the career center director concluded that the center needed to begin with a modest number of departments in order to have time to design, pilot, and modify the processes it used with departments. Accordingly, an initial group of nine departments and programs was targeted: teacher education, mathematics, chemistry, business and technology education, marketing, accounting, history, occupational therapy, and the honors program. The selection of departments was left to individual staff members, who generally chose departments they felt would be especially amenable to piloting the approach. At this writing, meetings are still under way in each of the departments to develop service plans, criteria, and prescriptions.

Experiential Programs

During 1995–96, a significant portion of the career center's effort focused on development of Web site access to information on opportunities for experiential education. Center staff concluded that for the Career Horizons program to be successful in responding to the varied learning needs and styles of students, it is essential to increase student access to experiential learning. Two types of experiences are viewed as essential: career exposure (experiences that permit the student to observe professionals working in the occupational field the student is considering) and career experience (employment and volunteer experiences that help the student develop and refine skills in the chosen career field).

During the 1995–96 academic year, efforts to develop increased student accessibility to both kinds of positions concentrated on identifying and categorizing on-campus student employment opportunities. Employing more than forty-five hundred students annually, on-campus student employment offers a wide range of jobs providing opportunities for career exposure, career experience, or both. Although many students succeeded through their own initiative in finding positions that provided those opportunities, no system existed for helping students identify all the positions on campus that might provide the level and type of position they sought.

Identifying and describing these opportunities required modifying the process campus employers used to post vacancies, to require them to more clearly identify for each position the skills required to obtain the job and those to be acquired on the job; the majors and careers most directly related to the positions; and whether the position might provide opportunities for career exposure, career experience, or both. Further refinement in 1996–97 will make information on both on-campus and off-campus job openings available to students. In addition to its broader value in improving student access to information on student employment, cataloging the positions will make it possible for PCAP prescriptions to refer a student to job openings that provide opportunities for acquiring the exposure or skills and experience the student needs at that point in his or her development.

Web-Based Interventions

Even prior to the decision to implement Career Horizons, planning for 1995–96 called for the career center to devote considerable effort to the development of its Web page contents. Career center staff recognized that the student's PCAP could include links to information and materials contained in the center's own pages and other pages internal and external to the university. Eventually, students wanting to learn what someone in a given occupation does through their PCAPs could be linked to that occupation's professional association to view CD-ROM videos of professionals in action. The career center could expand its array of services to students by taking on the role of information broker, linking students through the prescriptions to the information and materials they needed—sources that could be tapped rather than developed by the career center.

What became apparent only after several months of working on the Career Horizons program is that being able to list both educational outcomes and Web-based alternatives for achieving those outcomes provides important opportunities for improving student attraction as well as student retention. Materials developed to enhance the retention and career success of EMU students can be used to reach students at feeder high schools and community colleges. In addition to providing those students with information and services that can help them with their career decision making and development, extending access to Career Horizons materials may be useful in providing prospective students with a clearer picture of the skills and competencies they will obtain at EMU. By working with faculty and career center staff at these institutions, before the students ever arrive on campus EMU can encourage them to set higher standards of performance and accept responsibility for their learning skills, career planning, and personal development.

The extent of Career Horizon's impact on EMU and its transformation to a learner-centered institution is impossible to assess at this time. However, by listing the skills students need to be successful and then providing Web-based sources of those skills, EMU is poised to take a major step toward mastery or competency-based learning. Acquisition of skills via the Web can be used in support of classroom instruction—and, for some learners and some courses, as an alternative to classroom instruction. The extent to which the PCAP and its Web-based prescriptions could constitute an alternative learning system seems to depend almost entirely on the willingness of the faculty to extend the process-identifying skills and experiences to include identifying the knowledge essential for success, alternatives for acquiring that knowledge, and means of demonstrating mastery.

Eastern Michigan University is committed to applying new technologies to teaching, learning, and research; and to continually interpreting and responding to a changing regional, national, and global society. Examine its mission statement and home page at their Web site (http://www.emich.edu). There you will find information about EMU admissions, financial aid, student life, academic programs, services and administration, and library and computing services. To find out more about EMU's learning technologies, conduct a search from EMU's main home page for the keywords *Learning Technologies*.

J. MICHAEL ERWIN *is director of the career services center at Eastern Michigan University.*

Before drawing conclusions from these case studies, we examine brief vignettes of other campuses. A number of colleges and universities have employed many of the same tools and approaches discussed in the case studies.

Vignettes of Campus Transformation

Donald M. Norris, James L. Morrison

Transformation initiatives can be discerned in a wide range of campuses across North America and beyond. The following vignettes are selected to illustrate the variety of such initiatives. They also prove that highly focused initiatives can have important symbolic value and mark the beginning of more significant efforts.

George Mason University

For years, George Mason University has been nationally recognized for its creative growth and development. GMU created institutes to achieve cross-disciplinary program focus and introduce new "cultures" into the prevailing culture of a liberal arts institution that began life as a two-year branch campus of the University of Virginia. By so doing, GMU created a multicampus, distributed, interactive university serving northern Virginia.

George Mason leveraged the forces of transformation through its new George Johnson University Center. Combining funding for two buildings, a student union and an academic building, GMU developed a vision for a combination student union, information technology or IT-rich study space, meeting place for the entire university, and location for innovative academic programs. The facility has the look and feel of an "academic mall." Its core is a three-story-high atrium housing a food court, bookstore, banking, and other commerce on the first floor, as well as the electronic library. Upper floors have extensive study space and docking facilities for remote computing, offices for student organizations, other dining facilities, academic program offices, and classrooms.

The University Center is a prototype of mixed-use space for institutions in the Knowledge Age. Students, faculty, staff, and visitors can engage in scholarship, work, entertainment, edutainment, dining, commerce, or other activities. This facility has become a magnet for campus activity and a mixing place for the entire university community.

One of the academic programs located at the University Center is the New Century College (NCC). In this program, students create their own self-paced degree programs and extensively utilize the tools of Information Age scholarship. The symbolism of NCC's location in the University Center is especially apt.

More information on George Mason University can be found at their Web site (http://www.gmu.edu).

Mount Royal College and El Paso Community College

The Society for College and University Planning (SCUP) has developed a workshop, "Making Transformation Work on Your Campus," that has been offered across North America to representatives from forty-five campuses. In addition, Mount Royal College (in Calgary, Alberta) and El Paso Community College (Texas) brought SCUP's workshops to their campuses to involve a broad cross section of the campus in dialogue on transformation.

Mount Royal College, a public college, staged a two-day series of discussions among the SCUP team; faculty, staff, and students at the college; and stakeholders from the local community. Over the course of the two-day period, more than 250 people were involved. The dialogue will be continued by the campus through participation in an ongoing "collaboratory," open to all the campuses that have engaged in the SCUP workshop program. Mount Royal College plans to use the insights from these dialogues to shape its campus planning in response to several provincial funding initiatives for learning enhancement, infrastructure renewal, and performance-based funding. More information on Mount Royal College can be found at their Web site (http://www.mtroyal.ab.ca).

El Paso Community College is one of the institutions competitively selected to participate in the American Council for Education (ACE) institutional change program. It staged a two-day dialogue between the SCUP team and the seventy-five people most involved in the ACE program. El Paso Community College will also participate in the collaboratory dialogue, combining the resulting insights with those from the ACE program. More information on El Paso Community College can be found at their Web site (http://www.epcc.edu).

The ACE Program, the Pew Foundation's Campus Roundtables, and the American Association for Higher Education's (AAHE) Roundtables on Technology in Teaching and Learning are other examples of programs designed to provoke ongoing campus dialogues on transformation.

Georgia Institute of Technology

Georgia Institute of Technology has been pursuing a vision of becoming the prototypical technological university for the twenty-first century.

One of the mechanisms for redirecting its programs and processes was provided by the Georgia Tech Foundation (GTF). The GTF provides over $10 million per year in support to Georgia Tech in a variety of programmatic areas, both administrative and academic. To ensure that these investments were being used strategically, the GTF used a third-party evaluator to review the programs and the nature of GTF's support. The results were used to guide GTF's future allocation of funding and to strategically reshape a number of programs in a more strategic and leveraged direction.

Further information on Georgia Tech can be found at their Web site (http://www.gatech.edu).

Regis University

Regis University, Denver, Colorado, is a leader in developing accelerated learning programs for adult learners. It has established comprehensive learning partnerships with a number of major corporations, to link workplace and learning. In addition, Regis has formed a collaborative network to share innovative learning ideas and approaches with institutions applying the techniques on their campuses. Regis has created an innovative New Venture Group (NVG) that is its learning R&D unit. The NVG generates a substantial profit every year through its new programs and is a creative mechanism for creating a future-oriented learning vision for Regis University and its participating educational partners.

The newest set of challenges for Regis is how to leverage these efforts in the face of developments in corporate learning, that is, the emergence of perpetual learning that fuses work and learning at the desktop. These new developments are being assessed by the New Ventures Group for inclusion in the new generation of initiatives.

More information on Regis University can be found at their Web site (http://www.regis.edu).

Northern Illinois University

Northern Illinois University (NIU) is redirecting its development and institutional advancement processes to be a greater agent of transformation. The theme is simple: advancement and fundraising can be used much more effectively than is currently the norm to raise money for investment in IT infrastructure. By developing specific fundraising initiatives that involve use of IT as a transformative tool, and by pitching these initiatives to potential donors with an interest in the IT industry and in using technology to transform learning, NIU hopes to increase the total funds raised and direct a large share to transformational initiatives.

For example, a donor who has profited from the technology business and would ordinarily give the university a $20,000 donation might be inclined to give $2 million to a creative, instructive program designed to use technology to increase the effectiveness of learning. The donor might create an endowment for pools of instructional development specialists, or for graduate students to develop learningware. These concepts are being utilized to redirect the institutional advancement program; NIU is rolling out new initiatives in its next campaign.

More information on Northern Illinois University can be found at their Web site (http://www.niu.edu).

Northern Arizona University

Northern Arizona University is a nationally recognized leader in the use of distance learning. Its distance learning network essentially serves as a "utility" for the state of Arizona to reach learners all over the state, including those on American Indian reservations. It also serves other state agency needs. The faculty have developed extensive experience in redesigning instructional techniques to use two-way audio and two-way video technologies.

Northern Arizona is now pursuing means to leverage these efforts and its virtual instructional development capabilities to create new learning tools that can be made part of the Western Governors' University.

More information on Northern Arizona University can be found at their Web site (http://www.nau.edu).

Université de Montreal

The Université de Montreal is using the challenge of retrenchment to refocus its efforts. Colleges and universities in Quebec are dramatically reducing their budgets. The University of Montreal is transforming its academic activities to achieve fiscal balance, realign and modulate faculty and departmental missions, redefine disciplinary responsibilities, and reconfigure the various disciplinary sectors. These goals are being pursued through an ongoing campus planning initiative.

DONALD M. NORRIS *is president of Strategic Initiatives, a management consulting firm located in Herndon, Virginia.*

JAMES L. MORRISON *is professor of educational leadership at the University of North Carolina at Chapel Hill.*

*Taken together, the seventeen cases presented in these chapters yield
important insights on how institutions that differ fundamentally have
leveraged the forces of transformation on their campuses and beyond.
These campuses illuminate how to build assured migration paths to
the future, and how to develop the set of competencies necessary for
thriving in the Knowledge Age.*

What Have We Learned
from the Case Studies?

Donald M. Norris, James L. Morrison

The seventeen case studies in chapters Two through Eleven have yielded some
interesting insights about the acceleration of transformation. This chapter summarizes our insights on effectively using leverage points. It also suggests the
next stages beyond expanding the power of transformation: (1) creating
assured migration paths to the future, and (2) developing the capabilities
needed to succeed in the Knowledge Age.

Effectively Using Leverage Points

The lengthy case studies provide a number of examples of institutions that
have effectively used several key leverage points to accelerate the transformative forces on their campus. Six cases stand out as prime examples.

University of Delaware. The University of Delaware achieved a highly
transformative result without using the "T" word. In a sense, its leadership
used a stealth approach to transformation. The opportunities afforded by the
design of the new student service facility and the administrative software system were further leveraged through organizational restructuring and realigning the student service culture.

Virginia Tech's Cyberschool Initiative. The Cyberschool initiative
infused new resources and a highly visible vision into advancement of the use
of technology in learning, both on and off campus. The impact of this initiative was enhanced by intensive training of faculty across campus, investment
in the development of new learningware, and sharing successful models.

The University of Texas at San Antonio. UTSA leveraged the new
resources available for its new downtown campus, other new buildings, and

information technology (IT) infrastructure development by realigning its approach to IT developmental application. It also introduced a new vision for IT support of learning and learning in the Knowledge Age.

George Mason University. George Mason creatively combined funding for two different types of buildings to create a truly transformative, prototypical academic facility for the Knowledge Age. The impact of this facility was further leveraged by using it to house such creative new academic programs as the New Century College.

Lincoln University. Lincoln University used a number of transformative tools with representative stakeholders throughout their campus to involve students, administration, faculty, trustees, and staff to link potential developments in the external environment to internal decision making.

Arizona Learning Systems. ALS is creating a new learning enterprise. But unlike other independent virtual learning enterprises, it is fundamentally tied to the physical learning resources of the Arizona community colleges.

Most of these efforts are still works in progress, so their impact on campus culture is still emerging. Even so, it is clear that they are having a significant impact on their campuses.

Launching Parallel Change Initiatives

Transformative change is a circular process; there is no defined beginning point, and no end. In most of our cases, some defining opportunity or external intervention launched a cycle of multiple-faceted initiatives. Campuses that sustain ongoing, transformative change find that they eventually develop robust initiatives in the following six areas:

1. Vision and strategy for the Knowledge Age
2. Campuswide discussion and dialogue
3. Development of IT infrastructure to overcome barriers to innovation
4. Redirection of existing processes
5. Crafting of new learning processes and products
6. Creation of new cultures

Table 12.1 summarizes the role of the six parallel processes of change in each of the full-length case studies in this volume. The following discussion highlights some conclusions about these six parallel processes of change.

Vision and Strategy for the Knowledge Age. In order for a campus to prepare for Knowledge Age learning, the campus community should be exposed to a variety of visions of the future. In all of our case studies, campus leadership displayed some level of awareness that the Knowledge Age required a different set of visions and strategies. In many of the cases, this vision and strategy were still emergent. Several campuses had already defined and communicated the vision and strategy especially well:

- Virginia Tech's Cyberschool Initiative is an excellent example of a well-articulated and communicated vision and strategy for Knowledge Age learning that was understood across the campus community and beyond.
- University of Calgary's extensive use of a visioning process to position the university's strategies for the Knowledge Age is a model of a highly participatory visioning process that is ultimately being linked to program planning and resource allocation.
- UTSA's use of a Web site to display a learning vision and strategies for overcoming barriers to innovation is a useful model that other campuses may wish to employ.
- Lincoln University's use of a formal futures process to create visions and strategies is a comprehensive approach that some campuses may find useful.

The most important observation about visions and strategies for the Knowledge Age is that they are not static. Campuses that commit to leveraging the forces of transformation also commit to ongoing revision of visions and creation of alternative views of the future that guide initiatives and the development of infrastructure and competencies.

Campuswide Dialogue and Ongoing Discussion. Many of the case studies included a broad dialogue regarding vision, strategies, opportunities, and challenges. Not surprisingly, most of the cases cited above as displaying exemplary processes for shaping vision and strategies also had excellent approaches to dialogue and discussion (Lincoln University, University of Calgary, UTSA, and Virginia Tech). In addition, Mount Royal College and El Paso Community College were noteworthy for their staging of a campuswide colloquium and provision for ongoing refreshment of the dialogue.

A distinguishing feature of future dialogue processes is the use of Web sites and moderated discussion that involves a "diagonal slice" of the campus community in commenting on vision and strategies. The University of Calgary and UTSA case studies anticipate this new generation of campus dialogue.

Developing IT Infrastructure and Overcoming Barriers to Innovation. Development of IT infrastructure is a central element in almost all of the cases, either implicitly or explicitly. In the Knowledge Age, it is a key ingredient of every campus's vision and strategy for the future.

Several cases were exemplary in both their development of infrastructure and their overcoming the barriers to innovation posed by existing paradigms:

- The University of Texas at San Antonio used its learning visioning process to develop a future learning vision, pull that vision back to the present to highlight the barriers to innovation, identify actions to overcome those barriers, and develop measures to know how the campus is succeeding.
- Virginia Tech used campuswide training of faculty, resources for innovative applications, and publicity to build support for technology-enhanced learning.
- The University of Delaware used a new physical facility and IT infrastructure, new roles for student service staff, and new service norms to overcome barriers to one-stop student services.

Table 12.1. Classification of Case Studies and Vignettes by Parallel Processes of Change

Institution	Vision/ Strategy	Campuswide Dialogue and Ongoing Discussion	Develop IT Infrastructure/ Overcome Barriers	Redirect Existing Processes	New Learning Processes, Products	Create New Cultures
Case Studies						
University of Texas at San Antonio	Learning vision for 21st century and a new Downtown Campus	Learning vision process and Web site-based dialogue	IT infrastructure development, incentives for innovation, and training	IT infrastructure, campus planning, and facilities design	Distance learning and Web site-based materials	Technology-supported learning
Lincoln University (NZ)	Environmental scan-based vision	Broad participatory process	Subsequent planning	Planning, environmental scanning, and campus planning	Subsequent planning	Begin to change view of the future and lead to cultural change
University of Calgary	Extensive vision groups	Campuswide dialogue	Subsequent planning	Planning/budgeting process	Subsequent planning	Knowledge Age learning
Virginia Polytechnic Institute and State University	Cyberschool and Blacksburg Electronic Village	Campuswide training and application dialogue	IT infrastructure, Cyberschool training, and resources for innovative application	IT development and faculty development	Virtual classes, snippets of learning, and integration with electronic village	Technology-rich learning
University of Minnesota, Crookston	Mobile computing as a differentiator	Broad discussion	Mobile computing campuswide	Academic and programmatic planning	Mobile computing culture	Mobile computing
Arizona Learning Systems	Competency-based virtual learning linked to existing campus	Planning of new enterprise	IT infrastructure key to delivery	Redirect campus planning processes to reflect ALS	Competency-based virtual learning	New culture; part of new enterprise
University of Delaware	One-stop shopping for students and Web site-based delivery	Design team for IT infrastructure and student services building	IT infrastructure for student services and new roles and incentives	Faculty planning, organizational restructuring, and infrastructure development		Student service culture

		CQI process using Baldrige framework	Mobile computing	Use CQI to redirect all campus processes	Faculty professional development	Quality-driven culture
Northwest Missouri State University	Knowledge Age university dedicated to its region	CQI process using Baldrige framework	Mobile computing	Use CQI to redirect all campus processes	Faculty professional development	Quality-driven culture
Eastern Michigan University	Student success based on fusion of learning and work		New IT system enabled fusion of advising	Intrusive, consolidated advising system		Learner-centered culture
Vignettes						
George Mason University	Distributed university	Design process	Technology-rich environment	Combine two buildings to make prototypical academic facility for the future	New Century College, master's degrees in reflective practice	New Century College
Mount Royal College	Emerging	Campuswide discussion		Redirect campus planning		
El Paso Community College	Emerging	Campuswide discussion		Augment ACE process		
Regis University	New Ventures Group			Partnerships with industry	Accelerated adult learning	
Northern Arizona University	Emerging		IT infrastructure for distance learning		Distance learning	
Northern Illinois University	Emerging	Campuswide reallocation/planning		Development, fundraising		
Georgia Institute of Technology	Prototypical, technological university of the 21st century			Evaluation of major GTF initiatives		

As campuses develop IT and learning infrastructures for Knowledge Age learning, they come to understand the importance of focusing on the barriers to innovation and addressing them directly and decisively.

Redirection of Existing Processes. All of the case study campuses have redirected existing processes toward transformative ends. Every case could be cited for some creative redirection of an existing process or initiative. However, it is useful to focus on campuses that have used the redirection of a particular campus process as a substantial vehicle for pursuing transformation. Often, new visions and strategies emerge from those redirected processes:

- Northwest Missouri State University has utilized its CQI process and competition for the Baldrige award as a vehicle for building campus capabilities to become the regional university of the future.
- Eastern Michigan University created an intrusive, consolidated advising system for career, academic, and developmental advising and is using that system to transform its approach to student support.
- Northern Illinois University is redirecting its institutional advancement activities to take greater advantage of IT-based learning initiatives, thereby increasing both the amount and the transformative focus of fundraising and institutional advancement.
- Université de Montreal is redirecting its campus planning and budgeting processes to rationalize and transform its academic activities to achieve fiscal balance, realign and modulate faculty and departmental missions, and redefine disciplinary responsibilities.
- Georgia Institute of Technology utilized an evaluation of the major initiatives of the Georgia Tech Foundation to redirect GTF's funding.

Most campuses utilize redirection of existing processes, rather than launching of new processes, as the primary focus for transformative change.

New Learning Processes, Products, and Services. Development of new learning processes, products, and services is an element in virtually all of these cases. However, it is a key or defining ingredient in several instances:

- Arizona Learning Systems is developing a new model for virtual, competency-based learning that will be grounded in physical presences in all Arizona communities.
- George Mason University has established a reputation for creating new learning processes, products, and services such as its New Century College, its master's degrees in reflective practice, and virtual classes.
- Northern Arizona University has established a distance learning utility for the state of Arizona and created new approaches to distance learning for adults.
- Virginia Tech's Cyberschool Initiative, virtual classes, and integration with Blacksburg's Electronic Village is creating an atmosphere for perpetual learning.

The impact of the new learning processes, products, and services is substantially enhanced by other change processes: vision and strategy, campuswide dialogue, development of IT infrastructure, and conquest of barriers to innovation.

Creation of New Cultures. Creating new academic cultures is a necessary outcome of most of the cases. It is often derivative of the other change processes and takes some time to achieve. Cultural change is a work in progress.

Knowledge Age academic cultures need to be self-adapting, respond more rapidly than traditional academic cultures, and accommodate a broader range of learner needs. Such cultures are by definition "expeditionary": they continuously adapt to meet a heightened understanding of learner needs.

Campus change agents have found it difficult to change an entire campus academic culture at once. It is better to create new initiatives or programs with a distinctive culture suited to the particular vision, and then apply the new model to existing portions of the culture that may need to be changed. George Mason University's New Century College is a case in point of an expeditionary academic culture that is adapting to the needs of individual Knowledge Age learners.

On the other hand, change in the campuswide culture can be undertaken if the change process is customized to each academic and administrative unit, within some generally recognized campuswide principles. The CQI initiative at Northwest Missouri State University is such an effort. Application of IT to teaching and learning at Virginia Tech varies dramatically from one academic unit to another, but every part of the campus is included in the Cyberschool initiative.

Truly new learning enterprises, such as Arizona Learning Systems, should by definition start with new academic cultures if they are to be successful.

Building Assured Migration Paths to the Future

We have observed and analyzed a selection of institutions engaged in leveraging the forces of transformation. A distinct portrait emerges of many different approaches to preparing for the future, that is, combining planning, action, and enhanced organizational capability to change. These approaches include many short-term initiatives, but they are all part of long-term change processes. Although distinctive, these campus initiatives fit into some interesting, unifying themes:

- Developing new ideas, visions, and dialogues about the future having a transformational flavor
- Launching many initiatives, large and small, to leverage change and transformation
- Building personal and organizational skills and capabilities to prepare for uncertain, and very different, futures

This is not easy work for educators schooled in incremental planning. But new skills and capabilities are essential to the transition to the Knowledge Age.

The future is uncertain, however, and our capacity to understand it is poorly developed. In this predicament, we are not alone. Planning for the Knowledge Age teaches humility to leaders in every facet of our society. It also imparts new approaches to planning.

Planning for the Knowledge Age is like trying to climb a mountain whose crest is shrouded in mist. As we move higher, the mist rises, revealing new opportunities. The challenge is to move upward, guided by visions of what lies ahead, yet uncertain of the specific final destination.

There is not just one plausible future, nor one path to the future. The challenge of planning for the Knowledge Age is to prepare learning enterprises for success in a number of plausible futures. It also involves attempting to shape and direct future conditions to create the most desirable future. This requires the creation of "assured migration paths" from the present to the different plane of operation that will ultimately be possible in the Knowledge Age. These migration paths should prepare colleges and universities to be successful in any plausible future.

Extrapolating from our experience with the campuses we have studied, we find that creation of assured migration paths consists of several steps:

- Crafting shared visions of the future of learning, discussing those visions with broad cross sections of the community, and refining these visions continuously
- Bringing those visions back to the present to identify barriers to be overcome, competencies to be developed, and resources to be marshaled
- Launching incremental initiatives to build competencies and create assured migration paths to the future
- Taking decisive action when it becomes possible: forming new financial paradigms; establishing strategic alliances with other providers; and creating new products, services, relationships, and programs in learning and the certification of mastery

This is expeditionary development of new learning products and experiences. It views our learning initiatives and new programs and experiences as rapid prototypes that must be continuously changed and improved to move the institution up the mountain toward the future. We learn as we go, changing the prototypes to reflect our emerging understanding and evolving conditions.

From this process, we develop the competencies necessary to be successful in the Knowledge Age.

Competencies for the Knowledge Age

To thrive in the Knowledge Age, institutions need to develop five families of basic competencies, which should be present at both the organizational and personal levels:

1. Knowledge Age planning and change processes
2. Knowledge Age IT infrastructure and skill
3. New learning, interactivity, mastery, and productivity tools
4. New financial paradigms
5. Supercharged strategic alliances

The following discussion provides a high-level description of these competencies. A word of clarification: these are *basic* competencies, not *core* competencies. Core competencies are the few truly distinctive competencies that differentiate organizations from their competitors. On the other hand, these basic competencies are what *every* learning enterprise needs so as to thrive in the Knowledge Age. These competencies are acquired by the individual institution, whether alone or through strategic alliances with other parties.

Knowledge Age Planning and Change Processes. It is clear that the pace of change and the nature of planning and must be different in the successful Knowledge Age learning enterprise. Particular characteristics include the capacity to:

• Develop leadership skilled in leading campus communities in developing vision and accelerating change
• Engage in campuswide dialogues on transformation, change, and visions of Knowledge Age learning
• Redirect existing processes to transformative ends: strategic planning, facilities planning, new program and product development, campus governance, performance evaluation, support services, process realignment, and others
• Create new learning products and experiences to Knowledge Age standards of value-added, convenience, and timeliness
• Establish distinctive cultures in different parts of the campus and use new cultural models to change existing cultures
• Learn from successful leadership plans, strategies, and processes in other organizations

The capacity to engage in broadly participatory planning and strategy setting is critical.

IT Infrastructure and Skills. Learning enterprises in the Knowledge Age must be empowered by advanced IT infrastructure. Beyond the infrastructure, diffusion of skills in the application of IT will be essential. The Knowledge Age will be the era of end-user application of IT to learning. It will require the capacity to:

• Develop and sustain high levels of skill in IT application on the part of staff, members, and customers
• Network and enabling application infrastructure, plus end-user ownership of applications
• The next generation of IT systems, Web-based applications, and industrial-strength database engines

- Digital cash, smart-card facilitated applications, and other enablers of virtual commerce

Institutions lacking this infrastructure are at a substantial competitive disadvantage.

New Learning, Interactivity, Mastery, and Productivity Tools. In order to be competitive in the Knowledge Age, institutions need to develop the capacity to create new tools, products, experiences, and processes. These will involve all forms of scholarship: discovery research, synthesis, learning, and improvement of practice. Institutes must develop the capacity to:

- Provide and encourage the use of network-centered scholarship in all forms
- Create and deploy interactivity tools such as groupware
- Deploy mass customized learning management tools and scalable learningware
- Develop and deploy snippets of learning and learning agents
- Employ a variety of approaches to certification of mastery and competency testing

In the Knowledge Age, many of these tools will be developed by world-class providers and made available to other institutions and providers.

New Financial Paradigms. In order to plan, develop, and maintain the IT infrastructure and the learningware infrastructure necessary to achieve Knowledge Age learning, new financial paradigms are critical. These new paradigms:

- Utilize an investment model for new product development and for infrastructure development and maintenance
- Rely on a wide variety of revenue sources and cultivate new sources of revenue
- Place many educational services on a pay-as-you-go basis
- Enable payment for different kinds of value (intellectual property, interactivity, certification of mastery), and eventually online payment
- Involve venture partners and sharing of product profits with strategic allies

New financial paradigms are being explored not just in the learning industry but in every segment and society.

Supercharged Strategic Alliances. One critical competency for learning enterprises in the Knowledge Age is the capacity to engage in more extensive and ambitious strategic alliances with a wide range of participants: other colleges and universities, other learning providers and certifiers of mastery, technology vendors, media and edutainment companies, and corporate learning enterprises. Particular competencies include:

- Practicing aggressive, highly targeted outsourcing, cosourcing, and resourcing
- Employing partnerships in development of learning and interactivity tools

- Using new partners to acquire or access new skills
- Focusing on *core* competencies of participants in strategic alliances
- Sharing margin with partners and allies; coopting competitors

These alliances will create learning networks that eradicate previously impervious barriers between learning sectors and different providers.

Building Your Assured Migration Path

The transformation of higher education is a five-to-ten-year process. But our case studies reviewed institutions that are finding ways to unleash the forces of transformation. These cases herald the building of assured migration paths to the future. Leading institutions are taking the first steps along their paths to the Knowledge Age. The most important thing is to start—now, if you have not already—developing the competencies needed to succeed in the Knowledge Age.

DONALD M. NORRIS *is president of Strategic Initiatives, a management consulting firm located in Herndon, Virginia.*

JAMES L. MORRISON *is professor of educational leadership at the University of North Carolina at Chapel Hill.*

INDEX

Pew Foundation Campus Roundtable, 98
Program staffing (Futures Program), 20

Quebec, Canada, 100

Regional university of the future: academic governance of, 85–86; and Baldrige framework, 78–81; and faculty professional development, 86; and information and analysis for decision making, 86–87; and Northwest Missouri State University, 77–87; and seven-step operational process, 83–85; strategic planning for, 81–83
Regis University (Denver, Colorado), 99
Regis University web site, 99
Rio Salado Community College, 60
Rogers, G., 31
Ross, B., 29

Sargent, D., 47
Sargison, A., 19
Scanning workshop web site, 22
Scenario based planning, 24–26
Senge, P., 63
Seven-step operational process, 83–85
Shamrock organization, 12
Sloan Foundation, 44
Society for College and University Planning (SCUP), 98
SRI International, 25
State Board of Directors for Community Colleges (Arizona), 59
State-level catalyst for transformation, 57–65
Storyspace, 42
Strategic Futures Analysis at Lincoln University, 23
Strategic Initiatives, Inc., 10
Strategic Scenarios Group, 27
Supercharged strategic alliances, 110–111
"Sustainable Political Correctness" web site, 26
Sustained change: and academic department and faculty plans, 32; and coordination task force, 35; and current institutional planning activities, 34–35; and institutional committees, 33; meaningful engagement for, 31–37; mission statement and institutional development plan for, 32; and provincial budget reductions and the access fund,

33–34; redesign and change for, 37; setting context and direction for, 35–36; and strategic direction, 36–37; and University of Calgary, 31–37

TIFF funds, 13
Torgersen, P. E., 40
Transformation: leveraging the forces of, 1–6; model for process of, 63–64; strategic decisions for facilitation of, 4; support agents of, 4; transformation to Knowledge Age, 1–6; vignettes of, 97–100
Transformation tools, 21–26
Transforming Higher Education: A Vision for Learning in the 21st Century (Dolence, Norris), 1, 2, 6

United States Department of Agriculture, 41
Université de Montreal, 100, 106
University budget committee (TUBC), University of Calgary, 33
University of Calgary (Canada), 31–37, 103. *See also* Sustained change
University of Calgary web site, 37
University of Delaware, 67–76, 101, 103. *See also* Organizational realignment
University of Delaware student services building, 67, 74
University of Delaware web site, 75
University of Minnesota at Crookston (UMC), 47–55. *See also* Notebook computer technology environment
University of Missouri, 83
University of Montreal. *See* Université de Montreal
University of Texas at Austin, 13
University of Texas at San Antonio (UTSA), 9–17, 101–102, 103
University of Texas at San Antonio (UTSA) web site, 17
University of Texas system, 9, 10
University of Virginia, 97

Vice-Chancellor's Futures Group (VCFG), 22. *See also* Futures Program
Virginia Polytechnic Institute and State University (Virginia Tech), 39–45, 101, 103, 106
Virginia Tech. *See* Virginia Polytechnic Institute and State University

ORDERING INFORMATION

NEW DIRECTIONS FOR INSTITUTIONAL RESEARCH is a series of paperback books that provides planners and administrators in all types of academic institutions with guidelines in such areas as resource coordination, information analysis, program evaluation, and institutional management. Books in the series are published quarterly in spring, summer, fall, and winter and are available for purchase by subscription as well as by single copy.

SUBSCRIPTIONS cost $54.00 for individuals (a savings of 39 percent over single-copy prices) and $90.00 for institutions, agencies, and libraries. Please do not send institutional checks for personal subscriptions. Standing orders are accepted.

SINGLE COPIES cost $22.00 plus shipping (see below) when payment accompanies order. California, New Jersey, New York, and Washington, D.C., residents please include appropriate sales tax. Canadian residents add GST and any local taxes. Billed orders will be charged shipping and handling. No billed shipments to post office boxes. Orders from outside the United States or Canada *must be prepaid* in U.S. dollars or charged to VISA, MasterCard, or American Express.

SHIPPING (single copies only): $30.00 and under, add $5.50; $30.01 to $50, add $6.50; $50.01 to $75, add $7.50; $75.01 to $100, add $9.00; $100.01 to $150, add $10.00. Call for information on overnight delivery or shipments outside the United States.

DISCOUNTS FOR QUANTITY ORDERS are available. Please write to the address below for information.

ALL ORDERS must include either the name of an individual or an official purchase order number. Please submit your order as follows:
   Subscriptions: specify series and year subscription is to begin
   Single copies: include individual title code (such as IR89)

MAIL ORDERS TO:
   Jossey-Bass Publishers
   350 Sansome Street
   San Francisco, CA 94104-1342

PHONE subscription or single-copy orders toll-free at (888) 378-2537 or at (415) 433-1767 (toll call).

FAX orders toll-free to: (800) 605-2665

FOR SUBSCRIPTION SALES OUTSIDE OF THE UNITED STATES, CONTACT:
any international subscription agency or Jossey-Bass directly.